THE LIFE AND DESTINY OF THE GOD-MAN

JOHN MARINELLI

The Life & Destiny of the God-Man
Copyright © 2023 John Marinelli
Ocala, Florida …All rights reserved.

First Edition: 2/2023

Print ISBN: 978-1-0880-8920-0
eBook ISBN: 978-1-0880-8921-7

Cover and Formatting: Streetlight Graphics

Contact: johnmarinelli@embarqmail.com

This book is protected under US copyright laws. Any reproduction or other use is prohibited without the written permission of the author.

No part of this book may be reproduced, scanned, or distributed in any printed or electronic form without permission. Please do not participate in or encourage piracy of copyrighted materials in violation of the author's rights. Thank you for respecting the hard work of this author.

TABLE OF CONTENTS

Preface 1

Introduction 3

Chapter One: The God-Man Scenario 3

Chapter Two: The God-Man Continues 8

Chapter Three: The God-Man And The Voice of God 14

Chapter Four: The God-Man And You 24

Chapter Five: The God-Man And Dominion 37

Chapter Six: The God-Man Victorious 45

Chapter Seven: The God-Man And The 2nd Coming 51

Chapter Eight: The God-Man And The Day of Judgment 59

Conclusion 82

About The Author John Marinelli 84

Gallery of Encouraging Christian Poems 85

PREFACE

"The Life & Destiny of the God-Man" is a Biblical study of the incarnation of God into the human race, starting with man's creation, continuing with Jesus' and settling in the," Whosevers" that believe in Christ as the only begotten Son of God.

Particular attention is paid to, "The Beast Within", The, Born Again" experience and "The Battle" against evil that rages in every human soul.

Discussion is also focused on: "Taking Dominion", "Hearing God's Voice", "Living Victoriously", Spiritual Warfare", Final Judgment and "Walking In The Spirit"

The author has added specific encouraging Christian poems for the edification of the reader. Plus a link to 25 of his best poems set to music as a free download gift. See the conclusion page for the link.

INTRODUCTION

Being a Christian can mean different things to different folks. Some will say, "it's all about doing good." Others claim the name because it's popular with the crowd they run with. There are all kinds of reasons why a person will become a Christian.

Back when I was a young Christian, we had some folks joining our church and becoming a Christian so they could play softball. They learned to talk the talk but didn't go in for Bible study and weren't keen on becoming a disciple. They wanted the social life that the church offered.

After a while, it became apparent that they were not interested in being a true believer. After a while, they left the church and joined another that promoted a more liberal social gospel centered in the New Age philosophy.

As I grew in God's grace, becoming strong in faith and practice, I started seeing myself passing up other believers that had been Christians for many years. They lagged behind in Bible knowledge, faith to believe and even spiritual warfare.

I became alarmed, thinking that I must be off base or wrong in my thinking. However, when I went back to the Bible and read the words of Jesus, I knew that I was on the right path.

I was walking with the Lord. They were all caught up in the things of this world and had lost their first love. They began in the Spirit only to end up in the flesh. Their conversations were all about themselves and not their walk with God or divine destiny. They forgot what it meant to be a Christian. (See Galatians, chapter three)

Christianity has become, for the most part, a religion that can be set aside depending on the situation at hand. Here's what the PEW Research Institute report says about Christian Beliefs among church goers today.

The Pew report says that 15 % of all Evangelicals and 21% of all non-denominational Christians do not identify themselves as," Born Again" This report also says that 78% of all Catholics do not identify themselves as being," Born Again". Why is that important? We'll see as we continue.

The report tells us that *sixty-five percent* of all Christians say there are multiple paths to eternal life, ultimately rejecting the exclusivity of Christ teaching, according to the latest survey conducted by the Pew Forum on Religion and Public Life.

Even among white evangelical Protestants, 72 percent of those who say many religions can lead to eternal life name at least one non-Christian religion, such as Islam or no religion at all, that can lead to salvation.

Surprisingly, Christians also believe atheism can provide a ticket to heaven. Forty-six percent of white mainline Christians, 49 percent of white Catholics and 26 percent of white evangelicals who believe many religions lead to salvation say atheism can lead to eternal life too.

WHY IS BEING, "BORN AGAIN," SO IMPORTANT?

It's important because of what Jesus said, *"Jesus answered and said unto him, Verily, verily, I say unto thee, except a man be born again, he cannot see the kingdom of God."* **John 3:3**

It is obvious, to me anyway, that if you cannot see it, you cannot enter it. The question is, are non "Born Again" Christians really children of God? I think it is important to examine why Jesus said, "You Must Be

"Born Again." He was talking to Nicodemus, a ruler of the Jews of that day.

Being, "Born Again" relates to our divine destiny. We'll discuss this in more detail later in the book. I first want to lay a foundation by looking at the theology of the God-Man. This should clear up any confusion and answer a lot of questions.

CHAPTER ONE:
THE GOD-MAN SCENARIO

The concept of a God-Man did not begin with Christ, even though Jesus was the slain Lamb of God before the foundation of the world. (Revelation 13:8)

The slain Lamb of God refers to Jesus being chosen to die for the sins of the entire human race. It was known by God before he ever began creation. However, the God-Man concept began with Adam. He was originally created to be the man through which God would reveal himself. Genesis tells the story.

"And God said, let us make man in our image, after our likeness: and let them have dominion over the fish of the sea, and over the fowl of the air, and over the cattle, and over all the earth, and over every creeping thing that creeps upon the earth. So God created man in his own image, *in the image of God created he him; male and female created he them;*

And God blessed them and God said unto them, be fruitful, and multiply and replenish the earth and subdue it and have dominion over the fish of the sea and over the fowl of the air and over every living thing that moves upon the earth." Genesis 1:26-28

Note: Adam was a designation for the human race, (Male and Female) not just the male. (*in the image of God created he him; male and female created he them*)

"And the Lord God formed man of the dust of the ground, and breathed into his nostrils the breath of life; and man became a living soul." Genesis 2:7

Here is a picture of man being formed and filled with the breath of life, God's Holy Spirit. This completed God's plan which was to create man as a reflection of himself.

All of God's attributes would shine through man's personality causing him to join with his creator. All that would see Adam would also see God because the fruit of God's Spirit would bring the presence of God to earth in a reflection. Adam was fully man. However, he was also the temple of the Holy Spirit who, by the way, was and is fully God. Thus begins the God-Man story.

It should be noted that "Life" in Biblical terms, means oneness with God. You can exist without God but you are not really alive. You are a "Walking Deadman." Your spirit is not alive because it is disconnected from its creator.

Adam, at creation, had God fully present in him. You'll remember that the, "Breath of life" was breathed into him and he became a living soul. The, "Breath of Life" is the Holy Spirit. The result was the formation of "The God-Man" God and Man joined together in one place at all times.

Man's loss, when he rebelled, was the oneness he enjoyed with God. The Holy Spirit no longer dwelled in him. The Old Testament records many times that the Holy Spirit came upon the prophets and then left. He did not stay. Adam broke the connection, destroying the temple that was originally created for the Holy Spirit. The temple was no longer holy. It was riddled with sin.

Had Adam not rebelled, he would have become the source of Spirit-filled offspring, populating the earth accordingly. Instead, he did in fact rebel against his creator and lost his "Breath of Life" which, as I have said, was the indwelling presence of the Holy Spirit. This caused his offspring to be dead as well because of their fallen nature. The Bible calls this Sin because it is against God. (Romans 5:12)

Adam no longer resembled God. He took upon himself the image of

Satan and began to express the personality of that evil spirit. The Bible calls this the deeds of the flesh. (Galatians chapter five)

Nevertheless, his original destiny was to be the God-Man. It all started with him. However, the God-Man concept was not limited to Adam. His descendants were also chosen to participate in this adventure. Unfortunately, they lost out due to Adam's transgression. Receiving their own "Breath of live" was prevented.

The entire Adamic race was lost and remained dead in their own sin, detached from God and alone in a hostile world without the light of God's glory. They became subject to Satan's evil domain.

The human personality that was originally created to shine with the love and glory of God now projected the darkness of an evil persona. This evil image can be seen in our society today. It is full of lawlessness, violence, jealousy, selfish and all sorts of wickedness.

The Apostle Paul picks up on this new, "God-Man," theology to further clarify it and show its significance. He tells the church of his day, "And so it is written, the first man, Adam, was made a living soul; the last Adam was made a quickening spirit. Howbeit that was not first which is spiritual, but that which is natural; and afterward that which is spiritual. The first man is of the earth, earthy; the *second man* is the Lord from heaven." I Corinthians 15:45-47

He clarifies that the 2nd man was the Lord from heaven. That means only Adam and Jesus were chosen as prototypes of the human race. They were both chosen to populate earth.

The first Adam was to populate the existing earth. Jesus, the second man, is currently populating the New Earth that will descend from heaven at the end of the age.

The 1st Adan sinned, died spiritually and was tossed out of the garden of Eden which represented God's presence. As I have already mentioned, Adam's sin passed on to his offspring causing the entire race to be lost. (Romans 5:12)

This transference of sin from parents to offspring is not hard to understand. We only have to look at a mother that is taking cocaine while pregnant. When she delivers, she realizes that her offspring (Child) is also an addict. The drugs got into her DNA and were shared with the new baby. So it is with sin. It gets into the DNA and passes on to the children as they are being formed in the womb.

The 2nd Adam was the Lord from heaven that was the Lamb of God that was sacrificed, (died for our sins), rose from the dead, defeating all evil forces and secured salvation for whosoever believed in him. John 3:16

Jesus secured our salvation through a virgin birth, just like his own. "God so loved the world, (that's us), that he sent his only begotten Son, (That's Jesus), that whosoever believes on him should not perish but have everlasting life." John 3:16

You may remember that the Holy Spirit overshadowed Mary and she conceived, giving birth to Jesus. It was a supernatural (virgin) birth. In the same manor, the Holy Spirit overshadows the repentant heart causing its dead spirit to come alive unto God. This is also a supernatural (virgin) birth. The Bible calls it being, "Born Again." It is a second birth experience that creates an entirely new race of human beings.

The old human race was lost and dead in its own sins but the new human race will live because of Jesus. Jesus now dwells in every heart that has been, "Born Again." He does this through his Holy Spirit.

"And you, *being dead in your sins* and the uncircumcision of your flesh, hath he quickened together with him, having forgiven you all trespasses; Blotting out the handwriting of ordinances that was against us, which was contrary to us, and took it out of the way, nailing it to his cross; And having spoiled principalities and powers, he made a shew of them openly, triumphing over them in it." Colossians 2:13-15

So, the kingdom of God is now being fashioned for those who have been or will be "Born Again" They will not only be able to see a glimpse of it in this life but will fully experience it in eternity.

But first, we who are alive and, Born Again," must accept our rightful place as God's man (or woman) and reveal the image and likeness of God on this old earth. It is then that "Light" will shine into darkness even if the darkness cannot comprehend it.

Just so you understand, Light Signifies God's Presence and Favor (Psalm 27:1; Isa 9:2; 2 Cor 4:6 in contrast to God's judgment (Amos 5:18). Throughout the Old Testament, light is regularly associated with God and his Word; with Salvation, with Goodness, with Truth and with Life.

The New Testament resonates with these themes, so that the holiness of God is presented in such a way that it is said that God "lives in unapproachable light" (1 Tim 6:16). God is light (1 John 1:5) and the Father of lights (James 1:17) who dispels darkness.

Light is the revelation of God's love in Jesus Christ and the penetration of that love into lives darkened by sin. (1 John 1:5-7) Jesus declared that he is *"the light of the world"* (John 8:12; 9:5). Jesus is the incarnate Word of God, who has come as the light that enlightens all people (John 1:4-14), so that those believing in him will no longer be in darkness (12:46).

Paul agrees as he reflects back to the creation account: "For God, who said, let light shine out of darkness also makes his light shine into our hearts to give us the light of the knowledge of the glory of God in the face of Christ" (2 Cor 4:6). Through the Word of God, light came into existence (Gen 1:1-3) and through the revelation of God in Jesus Christ, the Word brought light to humanity.

It is this light that now indwells our being and lingers there until we decide to use it. Jesus said, "No man, when he lights a candle, puts it in a secret place, neither under a bushel, but on a candlestick, that they which come in may see the light. Luke 11:33 He also said "Let your light so shine before men, that they may see your good works and glorify your Father in heaven." Matthew 5:16

The God-Man began with Adam, was perfected in Jesus and now continues.

CHAPTER TWO:
THE GOD-MAN CONTINUES

Does Jesus dwell in you by his Holy Spirit? If he does, it's because God wants his Word to become flesh…your flesh and to walk this earth once again but not as a suffering servant but rather as a conqueror.

How does that sound to you? God wants you to manifest the life of Christ here on this earth in the victory that he obtained while in his earthly days.

"And the Word was made flesh and dwelt among us (and we beheld his glory, the glory of the only begotten of the Father) full of grace and truth" John 1:14

The "we" that beheld God's glory were the disciples. The folks in our day are also to behold God's glory but this time in us. (Glory means manifest presence)

It is important to realize that the "Word" spoken of in John's gospel is God's only begotten son. He was with God and he was God. Here's how it is stated in the KJV.

"In the beginning was the Word, and the Word was with God, and the Word was God. The same was in the beginning with God. All things were made by him; and without him was not anything made that was made. In him was life; and the life was the light of men. And the light shineth in darkness; and the darkness comprehended it not." John 1:1-5

The, "Born Again" experience is a supernatural virgin birth that brings us from death into life. "Jesus answered, Verily, Verily, I say unto thee, except a man be born of water and *of* the Spirit, he cannot enter into the kingdom of God." John 3:5

Born of water is the physical birth. Born of the Spirit is the virgin birth. It is the overshadowing by the Holy Spirit in which the breath of life is breathed into our souls, making us alive unto God. (True life is only in relationship to God)

Christmas is a celebration of the birth of Jesus, our Savior. We rejoice with family and friends. We take off from work for a holiday. We engage in intelligent conversation and go to church. It is there, at church, that we hear all the reasons for the season. Things like:

- Without his birth, we would still be waiting for a Savior, separated from God.
- He was born to die for the sins of the entire world.
- He was the Messiah, the fulfillment of Jewish prophecy.
- He is the incarnation of God in human flesh.
- He was the replacement of Adam for the purpose of taking dominion as God originally intended. (Genesis 1:26)

Jesus is 100% God…He is the God of creation and he is also 100% man…a human being like us. Christmas is the celebration of this event… when God became like man so man could become like God…. not a god or a deity but in the image of God, as it was in the beginning. (Genesis 1:26-29)

Listen again to what John says, (John chapter 1), "In the beginning was the Word and the Word was with God; and the Word was God. The same was in the beginning with God. *All things were made by him. Without him was not anything made that was made.*"

Everyone knows that the Word is a reference to Jesus being with God and is God, a member of the Trinity, long before anything came into existence.

Verses 11-12 of John chapter one says, "He came unto his own (The Jews) and his own (The Jews) received him not…but as many as did receive him, to them, he gave power to become the sons of God...even to them that believe on his name."

Thus, the entry of the Word, into human flesh was to open the door for many to become sons of God or like Jesus, 100% God and 100% man in one place at one time. *Thus, The God-man continues.*

If you object to this notion, listen to Romans 8:29, "For whom He did foreknow, he did also predestinate, to be conformed to the image of his Son...that he (Jesus) might be the 1st born among many brethren."

Our predestination by God the Father is to be like or in the image of his Son, which is...God dwelling in man...the Word being made flesh is not just one Son but many. Did not Jesus tell his followers that they would do greater things than he, because he was to go to the Father?

Now let's look at two images from the record of his birth.

- Born in a stable...a portrait of our new birth...Jesus entering into our hearts...both were dirty and un-kept.
- A Babe in swaddling clothes, helpless and dependent upon God to accomplish his destiny...a portrait of us...A babe in Christ, helpless and dependent upon God to fulfill his divine purpose.... to be Christ-like...born again into the image of God.

It's important to realize that pre-destination is just that, a predetermined destination. It does not mean that God decided to save some and damn others. It means that our destination (destiny) is to be Christ-like. That's where we are headed.

THE BODY OF CHRIST UPON THE EARTH

I am sure you can see more images just by reading the accounts of his birth and other related scriptures. The point is...the Word became flesh in the embodiment of Jesus. He opened the windows of heaven and poured out his Spirit upon all those who would believe on him so that the Word can once again become flesh, embodied in his saints…thus the Body of Christ appeared upon the earth.

TO BE CHRIST-LIKE

To be "Born Again" then, is to become the temple of the Holy Spirit who brings the Word to life into your spirit …thus millions of believers, full of God, a mirror image…endowed with power from on high, after that the Holy Ghost has come upon them…made in his image… to do greater things than he. This is the purpose for his birth and the destiny of every believer…*to be Christ-like.*

We know that Jesus first needed to be obedient unto death, even the death of the cross, before he could redeem us and lead us into our Christ-like destiny. If you want to see a portrait of your Christ-like destiny, read Galatians 5:22 and see all the fruits that belong to the Spirit of God… that is also the very nature of God, who Jesus was, is and will always be. Here it is.

LOVE, JOY, PEACE, LONGSUFFERING, GENTLENESS, GOODNESS, FAITH, MEEKNESS, TEMPERANCE…against such there is no law. Galatians 5:22

The story of Jesus' birth, life, death and resurrection continues in all of us who have been "Born Again". We are the Word made flesh to dwell among mankind as a shining light, pointing the way to God the Father through Jesus Christ, his Son.

Isn't this what life is all about? Isn't this the purpose for which we were born again? Isn't this the reason we are alive today…here at this point in time?

It's been said before that the only Bible others may read is you. The only Jesus they may see is in you…. so much more… the need to crucify the lustful affection of the flesh and walk in the Spirit…the fruit thereof evidencing its reality.

Some may ask, "How can I be Christ-Like"? I don't understand. Let me explain the process. As Jesus was born of a virgin, outside of the Adamic stream that was polluted with sin, (Romans 5:12), so is the Word placed in us…by supernatural overshadowing of the Holy Ghost.

As Jesus had to grow in wisdom and stature, so do we grow in grace. However, our growth is really that of the Word in us. It gets stronger as we are obedient to its call upon our life.

As Jesus had to deny himself, become as a servant, and experience death, we are also called upon to deny ourselves, take up our cross and follow him. The more we die to that old sinful nature, the more the Word lives and grows to maturity on its way to becoming incarnate.

"Then said Jesus unto his disciples, "If any *man* will come after me, let him deny himself, and take up his cross, and follow me." Matthew 16:24

Note: The Word in you is like a seed that needs to grow but you must make the choice to allow it to grow and even aid its development. How? By applying the written Word in your life. Read it, absorb it, live it, become it. Clothe yourself with God's Word until it rules in your life. To walk in the Spirit is to walk in the Word.

TRYING IS NOT THE WAY

Many Christians try to be nice, thinking that this is the way to show that they are Christ-like. Trying is not the way. It will frustrate you and lead others astray because it is not real. However, when you apply the Word, it becomes alive in you and the result is that others see Jesus.

Yes, they will still see you but they will also sense the presence of Christ in you and the Word that you absorbed, that changed you, will touch their lives and help them in their time of need. As you move in the Word, the Word will move in you.

Here's an example: You read in Romans chapter eight, that there is now therefore no condemnation to them that are in Christ, who walk after the

Spirit and not after the flesh. It becomes a "Rhema Word" from God, setting you free from guilt, shame and despair. It changes your entire personality from a sad, heartbroken, depressed individual to a positive hopeful excited person who is full of assurance and faith.

This change in you is not a, "try to be good" effort. It is a genuine transformation caused by the Word taking root in your heart and you allowing it to grow up in you by believing it. The result is Christ dwelling in your heart richly.

Only then can we see the Word made flesh and the God-Man continue. Here's a poem that expresses "Christ In You"

WITH EARTHEN VESSELS

Earthen vessels have never shown
such glory that once was known.
Through time and all of eternity,
came the glory of his majesty.

Full of love and full of grace,
He dwelt among the human race
to heal the sick, the blind and the lame,
to free mankind from sin and shame.

With earthen vessel he conquered all
by perfect obedience to his destined call.
For this we praise his holy name,
full of grace and full of fame.

The glory of his majesty
still shines through from eternity,
Again and again to meet life's call,
in earthen vessels to conquer all.

CHAPTER THREE:
THE GOD-MAN AND THE VOICE OF GOD

Is God speaking to mankind today? Is anybody listening? If God were speaking to you, what do you think he'd be saying? Is it too way out to say, *"I am hearing from God"?* After all, he is the creator of all things. He is the "Supreme Ruler" of the universe. Why would he want to talk to me? How do I know, for sure, that the voice in my head, that is talking to me, belongs to God?

We are left here on planet earth, seemingly, all alone, to fend for ourselves. It's a make it or break it existence with a future in serious doubt. Is that how you feel? I used to think and feel like that…like… Why do I exist? Why am I here at this place and this time? Do I have a purpose in life or am I just drifting with the masses towards an unknown destiny?

Well… I do not think or feel that way anymore. I was a teenager back then with very little knowledge or wisdom. It's been over 60 years since I felt lost and alone and without hope.

Things changed when I accepted Jesus as my Lord and Savior. He led me to the Bible and I, not only discovered my existence and purpose, but also my destiny. I realized that I didn't have to walk alone through a world that is less than perfect. *I found myself in God.*

As I searched, prayed and sought after truth, I began to hear from God. He started speaking directly to my spirit in ways I never knew were even possible. This divine fellowship, between God and me, proved to me that it was all real and that I was really a "Child of God."

THE WITNESS OF THE SPIRIT

I have already mentioned some of this, but it needs repeating again, Romans 8:16, helped me a lot because it said that God would show himself to me so I would know that I know that I am in him.

I FIND MYSELF IN GOD

> I find myself in God.
> He is my, "Everything."
> I know that He is Lord,
> My Life, my Hope, and King.
> I find myself in God,
> Not the ways of sin.
> Nor do I look to others,
> To know who I really am.
> I find myself in God,
> To whom I bow on bended knee.
> He alone is my joy and strength
> And where I want to be.

"The Spirit itself bears witness with our spirit, that we are children of God." Romans 8:16 KJV

Here it is in the World English Bible... *"The Spirit himself testifies with our spirit that we are children of God;"*

I am sure you are wondering how the Spirit of God testifies or bears witness. It's kind of hard to explain. There are so many little things at so many different times. I guess the most significant would be answered prayer.

When you are praying about a thing, asking for a specific result and he brings it into reality, you can't help but acknowledge that it was his doing. I have seen the hand of the Lord in my life, moving on my behalf; to deliver me from harm and bless me in ways that were so clearly his work of grace. (Read my book, "Times Past But Not Forgotten" It's a summary of the hand of God in my life.)

Then there's the Bible. You haven't lived until you read the scriptures and certain promises seem to leap off the page into your heart. You just know that the Holy Spirit is speaking to you and often it is concerning a specific problem or request. God's counsel and guidance becomes alive as you read.

CHANNELS OF DIVINE COMMUNICATION

God speaks to us in many different ways. If we are aware of them, we will be more ready to listen. Here are the three most important ways to consider:

1. **The Bible**…1st and foremost is the Holy Scriptures. This is where you discover God. his story, actions, character, and love are all clearly revealed. It is a great source of counsel and wisdom.

2. **Divine Unction**… The Holy Spirit will drop a thought or even an answer to a situation directly into your spirit. You will have a peace about it and you will just know that you know it is from God. This is, for sure, a non-verbal communication.

3. **God's Messenger**… God will often send a messenger with a "Word" of truth. The messenger could be the pastor of a church in a sermon, a Bible Study teacher, a Godly friend, an angel in a dream, a vision, and so on. However, be sure that the message lines up with the knowledge of God. It cannot contradict the truths set forth in the Bible. If it does, it is not from God.

If we desire to hear the voice of God, we must open our hearts. We do not hear with our ears. It is the heart that listens. As "Children of God", our hearts cry out for the living God. He is our Father and friend. It is his hand that guides us, helps us, and delivers us. He is the source of our blessings and very existence.

Many folks do not hear from God because they do not want to know. God, for them, is at arm's length and sought after only in a crisis. Day-to-day involvement with God is not on their agenda. Jesus as Lord is, to them, a slogan, not a lifestyle. This has been true for centuries. Here's what Jesus said back in his earthy days...

"He that hath ears to hear, let him hear." Matthew 11:15 He said this because they were not listening. They didn't have their ears attached to their hearts.

You have to have ears in order to hear but your ears need to be attached to your heart...meaning, this is a serious matter and it needs your full attention. You must be willing to take it to heart and act upon it. There are a few things you can do to make it easier to hear the voice of God. Consider these:

1. ***Establish a Quiet Time***...In today's self-driven world where everything is fast paced and rushed; it can be hard to hear from God. Although, your ultimate goal is to hear his voice in any circumstance. However, you have to start somewhere and a quiet time is a good place to meditate on the Word and listen.

2. ***Stop The Mental Traffic Flow***... The devil tries to keep our minds flowing with needless noise. As long as we are thinking about lots of meaningless things, we will not have the time to listen for the, "Still Small Voice" of God. Stop the mind chatter and listen.

3. ***Focus on God***...Seek him while he may be found. Don't wait for him to come to you. Engage in prayer and ask him to share himself with you. This will shut out everything else and clear the channel between you and God. This action is Biblical.

Here the words of Jesus... *"Ask, and it shall be given you; seek, and ye shall find; knock, and it shall be opened unto you: For every one that asks receives; and he that seeks finds; and to him that knocks, it shall be opened." Matthew 7:7-8*

4. ***Accept God's Will***... If we do not want to accept God's will, he most likely will not tell us his will. It is clearly revealed in the Bible. However,

he wants to share that with you personally from his heart. Obedience is the key to hearing God's voice.

5. **Call Upon The Holy Spirit**... We were given the Holy Spirit at our New Birth (When we accepted Jesus) It's ok to call upon the Holy Spirit to interpret our prayers, heal our wounds, and help us to hear from God. He was given to us for that purpose.

6. **Learn To Recognize God's Voice**...You can recognize his voice among all the other voices coming and going through your mind. It just takes practice. Here's what John, the apostle said... *"Beloved, believe not every spirit, but try the spirits whether they are of God: because many false prophets are gone out into the world." I John 4:1*

God wants you to examine every thought because all thoughts are not yours. They also enter your mind from Satan, The Flesh, Other's Expectations and of course, God. The one to act upon is the one that brings you the most peace. If you feel fear, anxiety, confusion or guilt, reject it and cast it out immediately. Do not entertain it.

7. **Be Filled With The Spirit**... God wants us to be continually filled with his Holy Spirit. This is a daily if not moment-by-moment process. We need to walk in his Spirit, live in his Spirit, and apply all that he reveals to us.

Listen to what Paul said to the Ephesians. "And be not drunk with wine, wherein is excess; but be filled with the Spirit; Speaking to yourselves in psalms and hymns and spiritual songs, singing and making melody in your heart to the Lord; Giving thanks always for all things unto God and the Father in the name of our Lord Jesus Christ;" Ephesians 5:18-20

Being filled is a "Be-Being" action verb... meaning allow God to continually fill you. In other words, one time is not enough. It has to be a steady flow of Holy Ghost power to keep you filled and ready to face the world.

WHEN YOU DON'T HEAR HIS VOICE

What happens when you just cannot discern which voice is God's? Sometimes, God wants us to use our minds and search for an answer. He will give us indicators and expect us to draw our own conclusion based upon the knowledge of God already revealed. Here are a few indicators that will help you to know if the voice you are hearing is from God:

- Is what's being said contrary to Biblical truth? If so, it is not God talking to you.
- Is what's being said causing confusion, doubt or anxiety? If so, it's not from God. God's voice always brings peace and has a tone of love and care.
- Is what's being said putting you under false expectations or oppressing you in any way? If so, it's not from God.
- Do you feel good about doing what is being said? If you are afraid and feel a sense of guilt if you participate in whatever is being asked of you, it's not of God.

Remember, the devil will always lie to you and suggest that you participate in some sort of immorality. It could be anything from telling a lie to stealing to even sex or murder. His goal is to tear down what God has built up in you.

God's voice, on the other hand, always encourages, builds up, strengthens, and is always in an attitude of peace.

MISSING OUT IS NOT AN OPTION

You should never feel sad about missing the Voice of God. Here what the scriptures say:

"So shall my word be that goes forth out of my mouth: it shall not return unto me void, but it shall accomplish that which I please, and it shall prosper in the thing whereto I sent it." Isaiah 55:11

God knows who you are, where you are and what you are doing. If he wants to talk to you, you will not miss his Word because he says it will not come back to him void but will accomplish that to which he sends it.

Jesus put it this way, "My sheep hear my voice, and I know them, and they follow me." John 10:27 If you are his, you will hear him when he calls.

The shepherd trains the sheep to listen for his voice among many other voices. That is what the Holy Spirit does when he bears witness with our spirit. He is teaching us to discern the voice of God.

"The steps of a man are ordered by the Lord, And He delights in his way. Though he fall, he shall not be utterly cast down; For the Lord upholds him with his hand." Psalm 37:23-24

God will order our steps, and even when we blow it, if we are truly trying to do his will, he will lift us up and give us a second chance.

KNOWING COMES FROM COMMITMENT

"Commit thy works unto the LORD, and thy thoughts shall be established." Proverbs 16:3

If our thoughts are established, we will know that we know what the will of the Lord is and we will already be in close communication with God, our Father who loves us. Paul tells us in Romans how to commit…

"I beseech *(Beg)* you therefore, brethren, by the mercies of God, that ye present your bodies a living sacrifice, holy, acceptable unto God, which is your reasonable service. And be not conformed to this world: but be ye transformed by the renewing of your mind, that ye may prove what is that good, and acceptable, and perfect, will of God." Romans 12:1-2

It is so much easier to hear when we are submitted to God and his will for our lives. I can remember a story from the Old Testament about a disobedient prophet. God finally opened the mouth of an Ass (Donkey) and rebuked him. (Numbers 22:28-30) We don't want God to have to speak through an Ass (lol) before we will listen. It is better to hear and obey and keep the favor of God upon us.

THE GOD WHO SPEAKS

God is a speaking, whereas idols do not speak because God is alive and idols are not. God himself is known as "The Word", and his speech commanded nothing to become everything (John 1:1–3).

"The voice of the Lord is powerful; the voice of the Lord is full of majesty" (Psalm 29:4). When God wants the dead to come to life he says, "Live!" (Ezekiel 16:6), and when Jesus wanted his friend to walk out of the grave, he spoke, "Lazarus, come forth" (John 11:43). Even now, Jesus is holding together your molecules with his words (Hebrews 1:3). If Jesus were to stop speaking, we would stop existing.

A STILL SMALL VOICE

There is only one place in Scripture where God is said to have spoken in a *"Still Small Voice,"* It was to Elijah after his dramatic victory over the prophets of Baal (1 Kings 18:20-40;

God is not confined to a single manner of communicating. Elsewhere in Scripture, he is said to communicate through a whirlwind (Job 38:1), to announce his presence by an earthquake (Exodus 19:18), and to speak in a voice that sounds like thunder (1 Samuel 2:10; Job 37:2; Psalm 104:7; John 12:29). In Psalm 77:18 his voice is compared to both thunder and a whirlwind and in Revelation 4:5, we're told that lightning and thunder proceed from the throne in heaven.

Nor is God limited to natural phenomena when he speaks. All through the Old Testament, he speaks through his prophets. The common thread in all the prophets is the phrase, *"Thus says the Lord."* He speaks through the writers of Scripture. Most graciously, however, he speaks through his Son, the Lord Jesus. The writer to the Hebrews opens his letter with this truth:

"Long ago, at many times and in many ways, God spoke to our fathers by the prophets, but in these last days he has spoken to us by his Son, whom he appointed the heir of all things, through whom also he created the world" (Hebrews 1:1–2).

Hebrews 1:1-2 tells us that the voice we are hearing is the voice of Jesus. Hebrews says this… *"Keep your lives free from the love of money and be content with what you have*, because God has said, "Never will I leave you; never will I forsake you. So, we say with confidence, "The Lord is my helper; I will not be afraid. What can mere mortals do to me? Hebrews 13:5-6 NIV

It is less important to know how God speaks to us than it is to know what we should do with what he says. God speaks most clearly to us in our day through his Word. The more we learn it, the more ready we will be to recognize his voice when he speaks, and the more likely we are to obey what we hear.

Let's summarize so we are all on the same page. Here's some of what we know so far:

1. God's Word will find you and accomplish everything he wanted. It will not return to him void or empty.
2. We need to be filled with the Holy Spirit continually so as to benefit from His gifts and walk with him through life's every trial.
3. A "Quiet Time" is a good place to start listening for God's voice.
4. God is not restricted to a "Still Small Voice." He can shout with the voice of thunder if he needs to.
5. We are encouraged to try or test the spirits (Thoughts) that enter our minds to be sure they are of God.
6. The Bible is the life-source of all revelation and knowledge of God. Every thought must line up with its truth.

7. The more we are committed to doing God's Will, the easier it will be to hear his voice.
8. When we cannot discern the voice of God in a situation, we should look for indicators, Bible knowledge, that we already know and use it to approve or reject the voice in our head.
9. The Spirit of God will bear witness with our spirit that we are his children.
10. Don't wait for something to happen. ***"Ask, Knock & Seek"*** the Lord until heaven opens and you hear his voice. This is his Will that you do so.

CHAPTER FOUR:
THE GOD-MAN AND YOU

"What? know ye not that your body is the temple of the Holy Ghost *which is* in you, which ye have of God, and ye are not your own?" "For ye are bought with a price: therefore, glorify God in your body and in your spirit which are God's." I Corinthians 6:19-20 (What was the price? The precious Blood of Jesus)

CHRIST IN YOU...THE HOPE OF GLORY

"I beseech you therefore, brethren, by the mercies of God, that ye present your bodies a living sacrifice, holy, acceptable unto God, which is your reasonable service. And be not conformed to this world: but be ye *transformed* by the renewing of your mind, that ye may prove what is that good, and acceptable, and perfect, will of God." Romans 12:1-2

Your transformation will have a profound effect on others who know you and yet see Jesus. This is Christ in you...the hope of glory. This is to be Christ-like. This is the process of transformation into the image of God's only Son. This is the life in abundance spoken of by Jesus in John 10:10. This is what Christianity is all about. This is the Word being manifested in human flesh.

Life is now a celebration that occurs when we open our hearts to the infilling of his Spirit.

Did you see it? The transformation into the image of Christ happens when we renew our minds. All that is; is gaining a new perspective.

The word, *perspective,* according to the dictionary, means, a particular attitude toward or way of regarding something; a point of view: If your point of view on abortion is that it is ok to destroy the unborn and you change your mind, now thinking that abortion is a sin against God and life itself, you have obtained a new perspective. This is how you renew your mind. Do this with all aspects of life and you will be transformed from liberal to conservative; evil to good; Selfish to generous and so on.

The spiritual application is found in Galatians chapter five. This is where the apostle Paul contrasts the fruit of the Spirit with the deeds of the flesh. If we cast off the deeds of the flesh and embrace the fruit of the Spirit, we have successfully renewed our minds and enabled the transformation from death into life to take place. This is how we become Christ-like.

Take note of your emotions. Are you frequently angry? If you cast off that anger replacing it with longsuffering, you dawn a new perspective. You now are demonstrating the very nature of God. Is this easy to do? Not at all. It is very hard because your base nature, (The Flesh), is evil and filled with anger if it doesn't get its way.

We have to deny it access; reject it and do not give it opportunity to express itself in and through us. Then we pray for patience and the ability to reveal Christ's nature. Yes, it is hard but you can accomplish it by dying to your own will and allowing the Holy Spirit to fill you with God's love. Practice makes perfect.

Why can't folks see Jesus in you? Jesus said, "**Let your light so shine** before men, that they may see **your** good works, and glorify **your** Father which is in heaven." Matthew 5:16

All we really have to do is open our hearts and let the light of God's love shine forth. It will automatically produce good works that will catch the attention of those around us. They will have no other choice but to glorify God. They will surely see Jesus in you.

Question? If the Holy Spirit dwells in you and your body is the temple of the Holy Spirit, shouldn't he be seated on the throne of your life? Most folks, including Christians, are seated as god on the throne of their own lives. They do not even consult with the Spirit of God on issues of concern.

The Bible tells us, **"Dear little children, you are from God and have overcome them, because the one who is in you is greater than the one who is in the world"** (1 John 4:4).

John is telling his followers that because they are the temple of the Holy Spirit and he is dwelling inside of them, that he, (the Holy Spirit) is greater that he, (the many anti-Christs,) that are in the world.

You'll remember that God is all powerful. I can only surmise that all that power is in me and it is so great that the glory of God encompasses me and his love flows out of my being defeating any and all foes. All I have to do is seek God's Will over and above my own. His Will is always first. This is in every situation, no matter if it is buying a new car, moving from one location to another or whatever. Seeking God's Will keeps Jesus on the throne of our lives and ensures our divine destiny.

I know what you are about to say, "How can I truly know God's Will?" There is an easy way to know that you know God's Will. It is to read the scriptures, the Bible.

KNOWING THAT YOU KNOW

If you call yourself a Child of God, you should agree with me that you ought to know the Will of your Heavenly Father. You are openly admitting to a relationship and claiming family rights and access. Are we in agreement so far?

Knowing God is a logical assumption when we claim to be his child. Yet most of the Christians I know have serious doubts about the "Will of God" for them. This can only mean one of two things:

1. Your relationship with God the Father is not a close one. You pray, he listens, but you rarely feel his presence or hear his voice….or

2. You have claimed to be a child of God but really are not. You know there is something not right but are too ashamed or afraid to openly admit to not being a child of God.

In either case mentioned above, there is a way to "know that you know" so there is no more doubt. However, knowing that you know takes faith. God is speaking all the time through the Bible, through his Spirit and through other folks that he brings into your life. The quick fix to "Knowing That You Know" is to "Listen and Believe".

I can say, without a doubt, that I know the Will of God for my life. I can make such a claim because my Heavenly Father has published 66 books that contain over 3,000 promises and many great statements as to what his Will is for his children. It's all there in the Bible, just waiting for me to dig it out, **"Listen and Believe".**

To know that you know is a great feeling because there is no more anxiety. I know and have been persuaded that this way is the right way and my new perspective brings me a lot of comfort, peace and hope for the future.

"And thine ears shall hear a word behind thee, saying, this is the way, walk ye in it, when ye turn to the right hand, and when ye turn to the left." Isaiah 30:21

The Bible says, "For ye have not received the spirit of bondage again to fear; but ye have received the Spirit of adoption, whereby we cry, Abba, (which means), Father. The Spirit itself bears witness with our spirit, that we are the children of God: And if children, then heirs; heirs of God, and joint-heirs with Christ; if so be that we suffer with him, that we may be also glorified together." Romans 8:15-17

As the scripture says, the Spirit of God will bear witness with our spirits that we are the children of God. If you've ever felt, seen or otherwise realized the witness of God's Spirit, you will know without a shadow of a doubt, that you are a child of God.... and if a child also a joint-heir with Christ.

HOW DOES THE HOLY SPIRIT BEAR WITNESS WITH OUR SPIRIT?

Notice that the apostle Paul *didn't* say that the Spirit bears witness with our flesh, our souls or minds. He *didn't* say the witness would be through the intellect. He said the witness would be from ***Spirit to spirit.***

That means it could be one of many gentle quiet assurances that we did the right thing at the right time. It could be a sense of stability when things are going rough. It could be, an "I just know" feeling. The point here is that God's Spirit is talking to us and our spirit is listening and rejoicing that it can hear God when he speaks.

One definite witness, that I can recall, is when I read the scriptures, they started jumping off the page with new and fresh revelation. The Bible, all of a sudden, came alive and spoke directly to my spirit. God's Holy Spirit was and is still confirming to me that I am a child of the Living God.

So, we have a quiet assurance and a loud voice that calls us to the Word of God, where we receive faith, instruction, correction, assurance, strength, knowledge and a lot more. God's witness is everywhere.

Here's what Jesus said, "If any man will do his will, (God's Will), he shall know of the doctrine, whether it be of God, or whether I speak of myself." John 17:7

We have to be ready and willing to do his Will. When we are, we will know the doctrine or revelation knowledge necessary to accomplish the revealed Will of God.

Question! Why should God give us the knowledge of his Will if we are not willing or not ready to use it?

That would be a waste of time and energy on God's part and he just doesn't operate that way. He has, however, already revealed his Will in the pages of the Bible. If we really want to know, we can read and discover and learn and apply all that God has for us. So, let's look at the Bible?

I will take you on a journey so you can discover some of the great and precious promises that prove out what the Will of God is. We will look at several scriptures and discuss them.

GOD'S DIVINE WILL AS REVEALED IN THE BIBLE

1. *The creation of man…*"And God said, Let us make man in our image, after our likeness: and let them have dominion over the fish of the sea, and over the fowl of the air, and over the cattle, and over all the earth, and over every creeping thing that creeps upon the earth." Genesis 1:26

God wanted to create man, (Mankind or Male & Female). His divine Will was to create us. He did that in his likeness and image. Then he gave us dominion over the earth and all its life forms.

What does this say to us? Simply this, we were not a mistake, after thought or freak mutation of nature that evolved over millions of years. We were a specific and deliberate design that was created to accomplish the goals and objectives of God on the earth.

2. *The giving of authority…*"And let them have dominion" Genesis 1:26 The word, "Them" is all of us. We were to rule as the "Head" and not the "Tail." We were created to rule over the enemies of God, and all of his creation. When we are the, "Head", we are, as it were, the CEO or President…the guys in charge. Few Christians rule over their own reality. They are subservient to it and see themselves as the "Tail."

This victim mentality keeps us from experiencing the abundant life that Jesus spoke of in John 10:10. It is obvious that folks do not understand the authority that has been given to them by God. The greatness of God is in them but they either do not know it or do not use it.

3. *The road to follow…"**Jesus**, who, being in the form of God, did not consider it robbery to be equal with God, but made himself of no reputation, taking the form of a bondservant, and coming in the likeness of men; And being found in appearance as a man, he humbled himself and became obedient to the point of death, even the death of the cross.

Therefore, God also has highly exalted him and given him the name which is above every name, that at the name of Jesus every knee should bow, of those in heaven, and of those on earth, and of those under the earth and that every tongue should confess that Jesus Christ is Lord, to the glory of God the Father." Philippians 2:5-11

4. *The key to success…*"And let the peace of God rule in your hearts, to the which also ye are called in one body; and be ye thankful." **Colossians 3:15**

Dominion is the act of ruling over your world. The word "Rule" in verse 15 actually expresses the intent to "Reign". It also can be interpreted as "Referee" as in a game.

Paul is telling the church to allow the peace of God to referee any and all situations as though they were a game. By doing so, you can use God's peace as a referee's whistle. It will blow with anxiety, confusion, worry and so on to let you know that you are off sides and in need of a reconnect with the Holy Spirit to attain his peace and sustain an attitude of thankfulness.

If you find yourself in anger, worry or any other such attitude, you can automatically know that you have lost God's peace. God wants you to walk and live in his peace so you do not have to experience *"all that jazz"* of the flesh. It will kill you if left unattended.

For the God-Man to continue, he must know who he or she is in Christ and what authority has been given from God. What authority do we have?

One of the most powerful lies that Satan uses to defeat the church of Jesus Christ is, *"You do not have the authority"* to take charge and rule over anything, especially not evil forces. The devil keeps telling us that when Jesus ascended after his resurrection, he left us powerless.

This lie has persisted in Christian circles and has become a dogma that says, in effect, all that miracle working power ended with the death of the apostles. This heresy is now commonplace and believed by most evangelicals.

Question? ... Do you have power from on high to overcome evil by casting out demons, healing the sick, binding Satan from your thoughts or changing the outcome of a circumstance? Most folks are afraid to even try. They shy away from seeking the Lord for a "Word of Wisdom" or a "Word of Knowledge" that would help them to better know and accomplish God's Will.

Do you read the Bible, as it were, a history book? Or is it alive with revelation and truth that stirs up your faith and builds your confidence to act upon what is being communicated by the Holy Spirit? "So then faith cometh by hearing, and hearing by the word of God." Romans 10:17

What if I told you that you have authority as a believer? The same authority that Jesus had and still has is yours. All you need is to engage your believer and receive it. You can become the head and not the tail.

5. *The assurance from God...*"And the LORD shall make thee the head, and not the tail; and thou shalt be above only, and thou shalt not be beneath; if that thou hearken unto the commandments of the LORD thy God, which I command thee this day, to observe and to do *them*:" **Deut. 28:13**

You can live a victorious life. You just need to believe. How do I know, because Jesus said so?

"The thief cometh not, but for to steal, and to kill, and to destroy: I am come that they might have life, and that they might have *it* more abundantly." **John 10:10**

We can all agree, I think, that the source of our Spiritual authority comes from Jesus.

IT WAS JESUS THAT SPOILED THE PRINCIPALITIES AND POWERS OF EVIL.

"*And* having spoiled principalities and powers, he made a shew of them openly, triumphing over them in it." **Colossians 2:15**

IT WAS JESUS THAT DIED ON THE CROSS AS A PENALTY FOR SIN.

"For he hath made him *to be* sin for us, who knew no sin; that we might be made the righteousness of God in him." **II Cor. 5:21**

IT WAS JESUS THAT GAVE HIS FOLLOWERS AUTHORITY OVER UNCLEAN SPIRITS AND SENT THEM OUT TWO BY TWO.

"And he called *unto him* the twelve, and began to send them forth by two and two; and gave them power over unclean spirits;" **Mark 6:7**

It was Jesus that said, "And I will pray the Father, and he shall give you another Comforter, that he may abide with you forever." John 14:16

This other comforter is none other than the Holy Spirit that baptized the 120 in the upper room on the day of Pentecost.

Now Hear This…When the Spirit came on the day of Pentecost, he filled everyone with his presence and power. They spoke in other tongues and eventually went out from the upper room to preach, teach, do miracles and walk in the Spirit. Jesus did not abandon them. He sent his Holy Spirit to deliver his power and authority to his church and to became the source of continued power to live in Christ.

Listen to what Paul said to Timothy. "For God has not given us a spirit of fear, but of power and of love and of a sound mind." II Timothy 1:7

This is the Old Testament Word of the LORD to Zerubbabel: 'Not by might nor by power, but by my Spirit,' says the LORD of hosts. Zechariah 4:6

Thus, our authority is given by God, through Jesus and made accessible by the Holy Spirit.

In **Matthew 28:18**, Jesus said, *...all power [authority] is given unto me in heaven and in earth. Then he said, "Go into all the world and preach the gospel."*

Is there any doubt that Jesus has given this authority to us?

Luke 9:1, 2 says, "Then he called his twelve disciples together, and gave them power and **authority** over all devils, and to cure diseases. And he sent them to preach the kingdom of God, and to heal the sick."

Mark 13:34 tells us, "for the Son of man is as a man taking a far journey, who left his house, and gave authority to his servants, and to every man his work, and commanded the porter to watch."

Mark 16:15, 17, 18. Says, "And he said unto them, go ye into all the world, and preach the gospel to every creature. ... And these signs shall follow them that believe; In my name shall they cast out devils; they shall speak with new tongues; they shall take up serpents; and if they *drink any deadly thing, it shall not hurt them; they shall lay hands on the sick, and they shall recover."*

Clearly, Jesus has promised his authority to those who are his own. The problem is that we do not believe it, and therefore do not exercise it effectively.

Kenneth Copeland, A noted evangelist said this about the believer's authority.

I have authority over myself and my house. If the devil ever comes knocking at my door with sickness, poverty, lack, or oppression, I tell him, "Don't come to my house. You'll have to go peddle that junk somewhere else because I won't receive it!"

But I don't have authority over the devil in your life. Ultimately, you'll have to learn to stand against the devil for yourself. Of course, if you are a baby Christian, I can make my faith work for you. But in the final analysis, God will expect you to take authority over the devil for yourself.

If you've already accepted sickness or disease (or anything else the devil tries to bring your way), then you've got a mess on your hands, and you'll have to do something about it. But, thank God, something can be done in the name of Jesus.

Take authority over Satan, sickness, disease, or whatever the enemy is trying to get you to receive. Stand against it for yourself in the name of Jesus. Believers make a mistake by accepting what the devil brings to them.

You will be defeated if you don't recognize who is in you and the authority you have in Christ. By failing to recognize that the Greater One dwells in you, you will allow the devil to take advantage of you.

It's one thing for Satan to dominate unsaved people who are in the kingdom of darkness; they're under his authority. But Satan and his cohorts are dominating too many Christians who don't know their authority or don't exercise their authority.

That's why the believer needs to come to prayer understanding that all those spiritual forces have been defeated by Jesus. When the believer prays, he needs to pray from a position of victory because he is seated with Christ in heavenly places, looking down on a defeated foe.

When you come to prayer, pray from a seated position in Christ, far above principalities and powers, where you have joint-seating with

Christ. Jesus' victory is your victory. Because of what Jesus did, you are free from Satan's dominion.

Too often Christians just hang on and try to do the best they can, not realizing what their inheritance in Christ really entitles them to. Instead of taking their rightful place in Christ as victors, they magnify the devil and that gives him access in their lives.

You can dwell on the negative side of things and you will become what you dwell on. What you are thinking about and dwelling on is what you are believing. What you are believing is what you are talking about. Eventually, what you are believing and talking about is what you will become.

This applies in the area of demons and demonic activity too. If you think the devil's thoughts, you will become depressed, oppressed, and you can get into error or you can think on the Word, and your thinking can become enlightened, illuminated, and flooded with light.

Because I know Jesus defeated the devil, that's what I think on and talk about. Thus, the Greater One, (Holy Spirit), causes me to succeed because I'm giving place to God and the power of his Word, not to the devil. http://www.cfaith.com

Author's Note: So, to rule over our own reality (World) we are to:

1. **Put on the whole armor of God**
2. **Keep our hearts…guard it so no evil gets in.**
3. **Operate in peace to ensure you are always in the Will of God.**
4. **Rely on the Holy Spirit who lives in us, knowing he is greater than whatever we face in this world.**
5. **Realize that we are seated with Christ in heavenly places above all the evil.**
6. **Know that Jesus defeated all evil forces and we now are ruling in his stead.**
7. **Take dominion and exercise your authority over all evil that comes your way.**

Knowing your authority in Christ is part of finding God's Will. However, the best way to find God's Will for your life is not to ask friends, family, or anyone else. They are not God and often are wrong in their own decisions, which, if I am right, will show up in their lives as a testimony against them.

The best way to know God's Will is to ask God in prayer, stay in the Bible and look for direction, correction and guidance. *It's all there.* If you start a log of scripture verses and what they specifically mean to you, you'll have a history to refer to when you feel lost or confused.

Some folks might say, "Why should we Trust God, Give Thanks, Pray Without Ceasing, and follow all the other teachings of Jesus?"

I would venture to say that because of Romans 8:28**,**" And we know that all things work together for good to them that love God, to them who are the called according to his purpose."

God's Will is clearly revealed but only accomplished in the lives of those that **are called according to his purpose**s. We also know that God calls everyone to repentance and salvation (John 3:16)

The next pre-qualifier is **that we love God**. You would think that his children love their father. If they do not, it's because they do not know him. In any event, loving God is the prime directive.

Jesus said, "And thou shalt love the Lord thy God with all thy heart, and with all thy soul, and with all thy mind, and with all thy strength: this is the first commandment." Mark 12:30

The believer has the Holy Spirit inside of his or her spirit. He, the Holy Spirit, is greater than anyone or anything in this world that we could ever encounter. If we are walking in the Spirit, we too have God's awesome power available to us to defeat evil forces. This "Authority" is freely given to us because we are a "Born Again" child of God.

We will need the power, "Anointing", of the Holy Spirit to overcome temptation and other evil tricks of the devil.

CHAPTER FIVE:
THE GOD-MAN AND DOMINION

Our fight is with the rulers of darkness. We are fighting because we need to defend ourselves. If we don't, we will become open prey for the forces of evil. Hear what Peter says in **I Peter 5:8-9**,

"Be sober, be vigilant; because your adversary the devil, as a roaring lion, walketh about, seeking whom he may devour: Whom resist steadfast in the faith, knowing that the same afflictions are accomplished in your brethren that are in the world."

Guess what? The battle is in our minds. That is where we stand or fall. We will still need the full armor of God.

" Put on the whole armor of God, that ye may be able to stand against the wiles of the devil. For we wrestle not against flesh and blood, but against principalities, against powers, against the rulers of the darkness of this world, against spiritual wickedness in high places. Wherefore take unto you the whole armor of God, that ye may be able to withstand in the evil day, and having done all, to stand." **Ephesians 6:10-13**

We will still need to guard our hearts. "Keep your heart with all diligence; for out of it are the issues of life" Proverbs 4:23

To keep one's heart is to guard it with all diligence. It implies that we should act as a gatekeeper that allows good things in and bad things from getting in. God wants us to protect our spiritual growth and resources. They can be depleted and even stolen by the devil.

Let's look again at Jesus and how he fought the good fight of faith.

Here's what Jesus did. "But he answered and said, It is written, Man shall not live by bread alone, but by every word that proceeds out of the mouth of God." It stands as our example and a blueprint for our success. **It is written** should be our victory cry when faced with temptation:

Jesus made the Word of God his final authority…there are many promises in the Bible related to walking with the Lord. We must discover them, memorize them and know them by heart. If they are the final authority, there is no discussion or confusion as to what to do. There is no compromise. We must also make the Word of God our final authority.

He used the Word in the moment against the attack. … When we are encouraged to do evil, we can use the Word to resist it, saying or repeating it to the voice in our heads or the voice of someone else that is telling us to do what we know is not acceptable to God. Your reply should be, "I cannot do that (whatever) because, It is written….quote or summarize the Bible verse.)

He did not entertain the illusionary lies of the devil… The devil will often create an illusion in our minds that is rooted in Lust, Greed, Pride or other fleshly appetites. He wants us to chase after the illusion and fall prey to his trickery.

However, the Bible tells us to," give no place to the devil". We can see that this verse holds power because if it Is written, "It Is Written" for our protection and use. We can speak it forth, hear it and obey it, knowing that it is the truth. There is no room for compromise. No room for "maybe so or maybe not."

He knew his authority in God and used it as a weapon…. Jesus knew who he was in God and stood in that authority. Most of us do not know who we are in God and fall into temptation and are defeated. We are the Head, not the Tail. We are Joint-Heirs with Christ. We can do all things through Christ Jesus. We are more than conquerors.

We not only fight the devil's fiery darts coming from outside our domain but we also fight the "Beast Within" commonly known as the flesh.

THE ORIGIN OF THE BEAST

The "Beast" was born out of jealousy and pride that led to disobedience. Its image and likeness are the same as the very character of the devil. He wanted to overthrow God and become God. ("I will ascend above the heights of the clouds; I will be like the Most High." Isaiah 14:14)

His original name was Lucifer when he served the Most High God in heaven. It was he that waged war against God and led a third of the angels into the war in heaven.

He is also known as Satan, the devil, the serpent, the evil one and many other names. He found himself on earth, with no power of his own. He had to steal that authority from man who had dominion over every living thing on the earth, including him.

We were to take dominion and rule the planet under the authority and grace of God. But the serpent deceived Eve and talked Adam into disobeying God's command. The result of their actions caused spiritual death to both of them and allowed sin to enter into the hearts of men and pass on through every generation. Romans 5:12 and Genesis 2:15-17

THE BEAST INVADES HUMANITY

Romans 5:12-14 tells us, "Wherefore, as by one man sin entered into the world, and death by sin; and so death passed upon all men, for that all have sinned: (For until the law sin was in the world: but sin is not imputed when there is no law. Nevertheless, death reigned from Adam to Moses, even over them that had not sinned after the similitude of Adam's transgression, who is the figure of him that was to come."

Romans 5:18-21 tells us, "Therefore as by the offence of one judgment came upon all men to condemnation; even so by the righteousness of one the free gift came upon all men unto justification of life. For as by one man's disobedience many were made sinners, so by the obedience of one shall many be made righteous. Moreover, the law entered, that the offence might abound. But where sin abounded, grace did much more abound: That as sin hath reigned unto death, even so might grace reign through righteousness unto eternal life by Jesus Christ our Lord."

Do I need to clarify? One sin brought death and one obedience brough righteousness. It's that simple.

THE IMAGE & LIKENESS OF THE BEAST

The image and likeness of the beast is exactly the same as Paul describes in Galatians, chapter 5 when discussing the works of the flesh. Hear what he said,

"Now the works of the flesh are manifest, which are these; adultery, fornication, uncleanness, lasciviousness, idolatry, witchcraft, hatred, variance, emulations, wrath, strife, seditions, heresies, envying, murders, drunkenness, revellings, and such like: of the which I tell you before, as I have also told you in time past, that they which do such things shall not inherit the kingdom of God." Galatians 5:19-21

The above list is only a partial list. Paul ends the list with, "and such like" which means there are more but what has already been presented is enough to make his point. All of these attitudes live within us and is what I call the "Beast Within" It is the very nature (Personality) of Satan.

We struggle with this evil nature every day. However, we were not the only ones. Hear what Paul said about himself,

"For I know that in me (that is, in my flesh,) dwelleth no good thing: for to will is present with me; but how to perform that which is good I find not. For the good that I would I do not: but the evil which I would not, that I do." Romans 7:18-19

Paul goes on to say that by the grace of God he can find deliverance from the Beast.

This brings up a theological question. Am I a liar because I lie? Or do I lie because I am a liar at heart? Let's see what the scriptures say, "The heart is deceitful above all things, and desperately wicked: who can know it?" Jeremiah 17:9

Jesus said, "Not that which goes into the mouth defiles a man; but that which cometh out of the mouth, this defiles a man." Matthew 15:11

The nature of sin, which entered the human race and passed upon all men, which is the image and likeness of Lucifer or Satan or the devil, whichever you want to call him, defiled mankind. He lost the image and likeness of his creator and now has to live with this evil beast inside that drives him to act out all manner of evil in the earth.

We can easily see this being played out in our society. Those evening news reports do not report all the wonderful acts of righteousness. They rather inform us of who murdered who, who cheated on who, how many burglaries happened last night, what political deceptions were tossed to the media and so forth. Evil! Evil! and more evil.

And what about the T.V. line-ups? The shows are the same, full of immorality, off color jokes, acts of violence and the like. It's hard to find a decent movie or sitcom without having to deal with bad language, violence, immorality or gay rights. We can clearly see the image and likeness of the Beast that lives within us. The work of the flesh is all around us. We are slaves to it and have no way out…or do we?

OVERCOMING THE BEAST

Paul tells the Galatians in chapter 5, "Stand fast therefore in the liberty wherewith Christ hath made us free, and be not entangled again with the yoke of bondage." "For we, through the Spirit, wait for the hope of righteousness by faith. For in Jesus Christ neither circumcision (meaning, following the Mosaic law) avails anything, nor uncircumcision; (not following the Mosaic law) but faith which works by love."

"This I say then, walk in the Spirit, and ye shall not fulfill the lust of the flesh. For the flesh lusts against the Spirit, and the Spirit against the flesh: and these are contrary the one to the other: so that ye cannot do the things that ye would. But if ye be led of the Spirit, ye are not under the law."

This is good news because it gives us weapons that we can use to defeat the beast.

The above scripture says:

The hope that is laid up for us in heaven, of which we have been informed by the gospel is something good, exceeding good. It is something future, which we are led to expect. It is something attainable, though its attainment may be difficult.

It is an inheritance that is incorruptible, undefiled, and that fades not away, which is reserved in heaven for us. It is a house not made with hands. It is a city, which has foundations, whose builder and maker is God. It is a state, in which we shall enjoy a freedom from evil. We will be put in possession of all that is good, both physical and moral.

This poor body will no longer suffer from pain — but will be healthy, spiritual, powerful, and immortal. The soul will no more be tormented by sin, nor harassed with doubts, and fears — but will be holy, confident, and happy forever.

This glorious hope is prepared for us by our Heavenly Father's love; procured for us, by our beloved Savior's sufferings and death, and revealed to us, by the blessed Spirit, in God's holy book!

The core of our hope is: The righteousness of Jesus.
A righteousness, which is the gift of grace.
A righteousness, which becomes ours through faith.
A righteousness, which Jesus wrought out for us.
A righteousness, which the Holy Spirit revealed to us.
A righteousness, which became ours by believing in Jesus.
A righteousness, which is imparted to us by the Father of Mercies.

How important then is faith in Christ? *Very*! Don't you think?

Being filled with the Holy Ghost does not exempt us from temptation. It does however; give us the power to overcome. The devil wants to capture us in "The Moment" where we fall prey to our own fleshly desires and where he rules the course of time. The Lord wants us to put our times in his hands and to be led by his Spirit.

The Bible says that we are not even tempted until we are drawn away by our own lust. Here's the Scripture:

"But every man is tempted, when he is drawn away of his own lust, and enticed." Then when lust hath conceived, it bringeth forth sin: and sin, when it is finished, bringeth forth death. James 1:14-15

The Lord showed me an acrostic that helped me to remember the offensive weapons available and how to use them to keep me free. This was when we watched the old-style TV sets that had all those knows for adjusting contrast, color, vertical, horizontal, etc.

Here they are.

1. **K-*The Knowledge of God***, "Casting down imaginations, and every high thing that exalts itself against the knowledge of God, and bringing into captivity every thought to the obedience of Christ" (II Corinthians 10:5)

We are to cast down imaginations and we could have many from sexual to being rich and powerful to almost anything. These thoughts are to be brought captive by obeying Christ and his word.

2. **N-*Name of Jesus***. "That at the name of Jesus every knee should bow, of things in heaven, and things in earth, and things under the earth" (Philippians 2:10).

It is important to know that every knee, meaning everyone or thing, must yield to the name of Jesus. In the name of Jesus, demons have to flee.

3. **O-*Obedience of Christ***, (II Cor.10:5) We must be obedient to the call and will of God. Rebellion does not sit well with the exercise of victory. Christ's obedience was exact and fulfilled the Law of God perfectly.

If we are obedient and we bring every thought in obedience to his righteousness, we destroy the evil thought before it takes hold in our minds.

4. **B-*Blood of Christ***, "But with the precious blood of Christ, as of a lamb without blemish and without spot" (I Peter 1:19).

Jesus was God's spotless lamb, a portrait of all the sacrifices from times past that were a foreshadow of him. He was the ultimate sacrifice. His blood forever paid the price for our sin. I John 1:9 says,

"If we confess our sins, he is faithful and just to forgive us our sins, and to cleanse us from all unrighteousness."

Knowing we are forgiven keeps us free from Satan's attacks that dwell on past sins. We can boldly declare that the blood of Christ continually cleanses us.

5. **S-*Sword of The Spirit***, "Take the sword of the Spirit, which is the word of God."(Ephesians 6:17.)

The Word of God is the Bible. There are over 3,000 promises and lots of wisdom, knowledge and help to meet all your needs. Use it.

Charles Spurgeon, a famous minister in the late 1800's and early 1900's, said this about spiritual warfare and Christians. (Spurgeon was called the Prince of Preachers.) He had the very first mega church in England.

Spurgeon said that to be a Christian is to be a warrior. "The good soldier of Jesus Christ must not expect to find ease in this world: it is a battlefield. Neither must he reckon upon the friendship of the world; for that would be enmity against God. His occupation is war. As he puts on piece by piece of the panoply provided for him, he may wisely say to himself, this warns me of danger; this prepares me for warfare."

CHAPTER SIX:
THE GOD-MAN VICTORIOUS

You cannot live a victorious Christian life if you do not know who you are in Christ. As I mentioned before, the biggest and most powerful lie that Satan uses to defeat the church of Jesus Christ is, "you do not have the authority to take charge and rule over evil forces."

If you dwell on the negative side of life, you will become what you dwell on. What you are thinking about and dwelling on is what you believe. What you believe is what you are talking about and eventually what you believe and talk about is what you become. "For as he thinketh in his heart, so is he:" Proverbs 23:7

This applies in the area of demons and demonic activity as well. If you think the devil's thoughts, you will become depressed, oppressed, and will fall into error. Or you can think on the Word of God, and your thinking will become enlightened, illuminated, and flooded with light.

I know Jesus defeated the devil, that's what I think on and talk about. And the Lord, who is greater, causes me to succeed because I'm giving place to God and the power of his Word, not the devil.

The God-Man is the head not the tail. We have already discussed this in a previous chapter. For now, I will just say, Be the "Head" as God wants you to be.

Jesus said, "Behold, I give you the authority to trample on serpents and scorpions, and over all the power of the enemy, and nothing shall by any means hurt you" (Luke 10:19).

God has given you all the authority you need to be able to stand against the devil and his works. He has also provided you with armor and spiritual weapons for your warfare against Satan. In his letter to the Ephesians, the apostle Paul describes these items and defines how to use them.

He writes, "Be strong in the Lord and in the power of his might. Put on the whole armor of God that you may be able to stand against the wiles of the devil. Take up the whole armor of God, that you may be able to withstand in the evil day, and having done all, to stand." (Ephesians 6:10-11, 13)

BIBLE REFERENCES RELATED TO THE BELIEVER'S AUTHORITY

Mark 16:17 …And these signs will accompany those who believe: in my name they will cast out demons; they will speak in new tongues;

James 4:7 …Submit yourselves therefore to God. Resist the devil, and he will flee from you.

Luke 10:19 …Behold, I have given you authority to tread on serpents and scorpions, and over all the power of the enemy, and nothing shall hurt you.

Matthew 16:19 …I will give you the keys of the kingdom of heaven, and whatever you bind on earth shall be bound in heaven, and whatever you lose on earth shall be loosed in heaven."

1 Peter 5:8 …Be sober-minded; be watchful. Your adversary the devil prowls around like a roaring lion, seeking someone to devour.

Luke 10:19-21 … "Behold, I have given you authority to tread on serpents and scorpions, and over all the power of the enemy, and nothing shall hurt you. Nevertheless, do not rejoice in this, that the spirits are subject to you, but rejoice that your names are written in heaven." In that same hour he rejoiced in the Holy Spirit and said, "I thank you, Father,

Lord of heaven and earth, that you have hidden these things from the wise and understanding and revealed them to little children; yes, Father, for such was your gracious will."

1 John 4:4 ... Little children, you are from God and have overcome them, for he who is in you is greater than he who is in the world.

Revelation 12:11 ...And they have conquered him by the blood of the Lamb and by the word of their testimony, for they loved not their lives even unto death.

Mark 11:23 ...Truly, I say to you, whoever says to this mountain, 'Be taken up and thrown into the sea,' and does not doubt in his heart, but believes that what he says will come to pass, it will be done for him.

Hebrews 4:12 For the word of God is living and active, sharper than any two-edged sword, piercing to the division of soul and of spirit, of joints and of marrow, and discerning the thoughts and intentions of the heart.

Acts 1:8 ... "But you will receive power after that the Holy Spirit has come upon you, and you will be my witnesses in Jerusalem and in all Judea and Samaria, and to the end of the earth."

John 14:12 ..."Truly, truly, I say to you, whoever believes in me will also do the works that I do; and greater works than these will he do, because I am going to the Father."

Mark 6:13 ...And they cast out many demons and anointed with oil many who were sick and healed them.

Ephesians 6:10-18 ...Finally, be strong in the Lord and in the power of his might. Put on the whole armor of God, that you may be able to stand against the schemes of the devil. For we do not wrestle against flesh and blood, but against the rulers, against the authorities, against the cosmic powers over this present darkness, against the spiritual forces of evil in the heavenly places.

Therefore, take up the whole armor of God, that you may be able to withstand in the evil day, and having done all, to stand firm. Stand therefore, having fastened on the belt of truth, and having put on the breastplate of righteousness ...

Matthew 28:18-20 ...And Jesus came and said to them, "All authority in heaven and on earth has been given to me. Go therefore and make disciples of all nations, baptizing them in the name of the Father and of the Son and of the Holy Spirit, teaching them to observe all that I have commanded you. And behold, I am with you always, to the end of the age."

Psalm 91:13 ...You will tread on the lion and the adder; the young lion and the serpent you will trample underfoot.

You have everything you need to conquer the enemy and become the head. Go for it!

THE GOD-MAN IS A JOINT-HEIR WITH CHRIST.

"The Spirit himself bears witness with our spirit that we are children of God, and if children, then heirs—heirs of God and joint heirs with Christ, if indeed we suffer with him, that we may also be glorified together." Romans 8:17

According to this verse, we share in the sufferings of **Christ** now and will share in the glory of **Christ** later as his "co-**heirs**."

Because we are God's children, we are also God's heirs, thus joint-heirs with Christ. One of the rights we are given as heirs to God's throne is an inheritance over everything that belongs to God. Our inheritance is not an earthly inheritance, but a heavenly one, and it is kept in heaven where it cannot be destroyed or looted. (Bible Gateway.com)

The God-Man Is A Child of the Living God...John 1:12 - But as many as received him, to them gave he power to become the sons **of God**, [even] to them that believe on his name: Galatians 3:26 - For ye are all the **children of God** by faith in Christ Jesus. Romans 8:15- For ye have not received the spirit of bondage again to fear; but ye have received the Spirit of adoption, whereby we cry, Abba, (meaning Father.)

The God-Man Is A "Born Again" Believer....*John 3:3-* "Jesus answered and said unto him, Verily, verily, I say unto thee, except a man be born again, he cannot see the kingdom of God." John 3:16-18-For God so loved the world, that he gave his only begotten Son, that whosoever believeth in him should not perish, but have everlasting life. For God sent not his Son into the world to condemn the world; but that the world through him might be saved. He that believeth on him is not condemned: but he that believeth not is condemned already, because he hath not believed in the name of the only begotten Son of God."

The God-Man Is Empowered By The Holy Spirit...."But ye shall receive power, after that the Holy Ghost is come upon you: and ye shall be witnesses unto me both in Jerusalem, and in all Judaea, and in Samaria, and unto the uttermost part of the earth. Ephesians 5:18-" And be not drunk with wine, wherein is excess; but be filled with the Spirit"

The God-Man Operates in The Gifts of the Holy Spirit...I Corinthians 12:4-11—"Now there are diversities of gifts, but the same Spirit. And there are differences of administrations, but the same Lord. And there are diversities of operations, but it is the same God which worketh all in all. But the manifestation of the Spirit is given to every man to profit withal. For to one is given by the Spirit *the word of wisdom*; to another *the word of knowledge* by the same Spirit; To *another faith* by the same Spirit; to another *the gifts of healing* by the same Spirit; To another *the working of miracles*; to another *prophecy*; to another *discerning of spirits;* to another *divers kinds of tongues*; to another *the interpretation of tongues*: But all these worketh that one and the selfsame Spirit, dividing to every man severally as he will."

The God-Man Walks By Faith… "For we walk by faith, not by sight." II Corinthians 5:7

The God-Man is in the Lamb's Book of Life…Revelation 20:12 & 15—"And I saw the dead, small and great, stand before God; and the books were opened: and another book was opened, which is the book of life: and the dead were judged out of those things which were written in the books, according to their works. And whosoever was not found written in the Book of Life was cast into the lake of fire. "Revelation 21:27- - then adds that the book of life belongs to the Lamb, Jesus Christ. There we read, "But nothing unclean will ever enter it, nor anyone who does what is detestable or false, but only those who are written in the Lamb's book of life. "Every person who enters the new heavens, new earth, and new city of God will be those whose names are written in the book of life that belongs to the Lamb. This is the same book of life mentioned in previous verses. This book of life was written before the foundation of the earth, includes every believer, includes *those who refuse to worship the Beast*, will have white garments, and will reign with Christ forever."

OUR GREATEST FAN

God is faithful
Even when we are not.
He watches over his Word,
Crossing every "T" and every "Dot."

He is a very present help
In times of sorrow and pain.
We can trust in his Word
For sunshine and latter rain.

He alone holds our future
In the palms of his hands.
He leads us as a loving Shepherd
Into green pastures and fruitful lands

God is faithful
To honor his covenant with man.
He, though LORD of all,
Is our greatest fan.

CHAPTER SEVEN:
THE GOD-MAN AND THE 2ND COMING

The Bible says that Jesus Christ will one day return to this earth. Listen to what the angel said to the men of Galilee just after they saw him ascend into heaven.

"Ye men of Galilee, why stand ye gazing up into heaven? This same Jesus, which is taken up from you into heaven, shall so come in like manner as ye have seen him go into heaven." **Acts 1:11**

Here's what Jesus told his disciples, "In my Father's house are many mansions: if it were not so, I would have told you. I go to prepare a place for you. And if I go and prepare a place for you, I will come again, and receive you unto myself; that where I am, there ye may be also." **John 14:2-3 (Reference to the new earth at the end of the age)**

Here's what the apostle Paul told the Thessalonian church of the 1st century.

"For the Lord himself shall descend from heaven with a shout, with the voice of the archangel, and with the trump of God: and the dead in Christ shall rise first: Then we which are alive and remain shall be caught up together with them in the clouds, to meet the Lord in the air: and so shall we ever be with the Lord." I Thessalonians. 4:16-17

The three scripture references above tell us that Jesus ascended into heaven to prepare a place for us and is coming back one day. I think it is about time that we look at what life will be like before his return and who actually will be caught up in the clouds in the rapture.

WHEN WILL JESUS RETURN?

No one knows when Jesus will return, only God the Father. Attempts have been made before to guess the exact date but the dates have come and gone and we are still here. So are those who made the predictions. Listen again to the scriptures.

1. Mark 13:32 – "But of that day and that hour knows no man, no, not the angels which are in heaven, neither the Son, but the Father."

2. I Thessalonians. 5:2 – "For yourselves know perfectly that the day of the Lord so comes as a thief in the night."

3. Matthew 24:42 – "Watch therefore: for ye know not what hour your Lord doth come."

4. Luke 12:40 – "Be ye therefore ready also: for the Son of man cometh at an hour when ye think not."

5. Matthew 24:26-27… "Wherefore if they shall say unto you, Behold, he is in the desert; go not forth: behold, he is in the secret chambers; believe it not. 27- For as the lightning cometh out of the east, and shineth even unto the west; so shall also the coming of the Son of man be."

THE CONDITION OF THE CHURCH AT JESUS' RETURN

The apostle Paul did not want us to be deceived. He wrote to the church answering their questions… *"Let no man deceive you by any means:* for that day shall not come, *except there come a falling away* first, and that man of sin be revealed, the son of perdition; II Thessalonians, 2:3-7

The great falling away is from faith. Folks still go to church and say they are religious but their theology has changed. Many no longer hold fast to sound doctrine that the apostles taught and even deny the deity of Christ. Religion is flushing but discipleship and true believers are not.

THE CONDITION OF SOCIETY AT JESUS' RETURN

According to Matthew 24, here's what will happen as we draw closer and closer to the "Big Event" which is the end of all things. These are the signs of the times that tell us if we are really in the last days before Jesus comes back and whether or not we are fast approaching the end of days.

1. Many shall come on the scene saying, I am Christ; (or I am a Christian) and shall deceive many. (Christ means "Anointed)
2. We will hear of wars and rumors of wars.
3. Nation will rise against nation, and kingdom against kingdom.
4. There will be famines, and pestilences, and earthquakes, in divers, (Various), places.
5. Many will be offended, and shall betray one another, and shall hate one another.
6. Many false prophets will rise, and shall deceive many.
7. The love of many shall wax cold.
8. And this gospel of the kingdom shall be preached in the entire world for a witness unto all nations.
9. As the days of Noah were, so will be the days before Jesus returns.

THE CAUSE-AND-EFFECT SCENARIO

One powerful example of cause and effect occurred in the time of Noah. The book of Genesis makes clear that "the wickedness of man was great in the earth, and that every intent of the thoughts of man's heart was only evil continually." **(Genesis** 6:5) The world then was "filled with violence," as humans corrupted themselves and God's creation. (Genesis 6:11)

This disobedience to God's beneficial laws caused automatic pain and suffering to the point that God was "grieved in his heart" and decided to start all over again through Noah and his family (verses 6, 18).

Even though, from God's perspective, the storm clouds of the impending flood were obvious, the people of Noah's day ignored Noah's warnings and lived as if nothing were wrong. Jesus Christ made this point in his warning to people about the signs of the end time. He said…"For as in the days before the flood, they were eating and drinking, marrying and giving in marriage, until the day that Noah entered the ark, and did not know until the flood came and took them all away, so also will the coming of the Son of Man be" (Matthew 24:38-39).

Year after year, human opinions about sin have changed. Actions recognized as wrong in the past are increasingly accepted, whether premarital sex, cheating, lying, swearing, lusting or homosexuality. Jesus warned that we must not fall prey to the apathy of Noah's day.

TWO KEY SIGNS
ONE FOR YOU & ONE FOR THEM

It's important to see that life is as usual before and up to the great tribulation. There are no signs or are there? Hear what the apostle John says, "even now are there many antichrists; (False Christians and Religions) whereby we know that it is the last time." I John 2:18

This is how we know that we are living in the last days…because of the many "Anti-Christs" that are in the world.

The other sign is the revelation of the Son of Man in heaven. The unveiling of his Shekinah Glory to this world. After the tribulation came the sign of his coming, being the glory, he exhibits in heaven and will here on the earth.

There are signs everywhere but the two mentioned above are the most important because of what they tell us.

Sign #1…Multiple Antichrists…The earth is full of antichrists that are hard at work trying to mislead the human race and Christians in particular. Have you noticed any antichrists lately? The one thing they do that gives them away as being an, "antichrist" is…well I'll let John tell you, "1 John 4:2

"Hereby know ye the Spirit of God: Every spirit that confesses that Jesus Christ is come in the flesh is of God: 1 John 4:3 And every spirit that confesses not that Jesus Christ is come in the flesh is not of God: and this is that spirit of antichrist, whereof ye have heard that it should come; and even now already is it in the world." 2 John 1:7 "For many deceivers are entered into the world, who confess not that Jesus Christ is come in the flesh. This is a deceiver and an antichrist."

Sign #2… Shekinah Glory…, which is the full glory of God. However, note that sign #1 is for us along with all the other signs. Sign #2 is a warning to those who are alive after the tribulation. This is pictured in Revelation 6:16, "And said to the mountains and rocks, fall on us, and hide us from the face of him that sits on the throne, and from the wrath of the Lamb:"

WHO GOES AND WHO IS LEFT BEHIND?

The children of God that have been "Born Again" are the folks that will be raptured from this earth and spared the wrath of God.

"For God hath not appointed us to wrath, but to obtain salvation by our Lord Jesus Christ, who died for us, that, whether we wake or sleep, we should live together with him. Wherefore comfort yourselves together, and edify one another, even as also ye do." I Thessalonians 5:9-11

The 1st century saints were admonished to take comfort in the fact that God had not appointed them to wrath. That would be his wrath that will be poured out on the ungodly. The great tribulation is when God pours out his wrath upon the earth. Here is another few passages to look at from II Thessalonians, chapter two.

"That ye be not soon shaken in mind, or be troubled, neither by spirit, nor by word, nor by letter as from us, as that the day of Christ is at hand. Let no man deceive you by any means: for that day shall not come, except there comes a falling away first, and that man of sin be revealed, the son of perdition; who opposes and exalts himself above all that is called God, or that is worshipped; so that he, as God, sits in the temple of God, shewing himself that he is God.

Remember ye not, that, when I was yet with you, I told you these things? And now ye know what withholds that he might be revealed in his time. For the mystery of iniquity doth already work: only he who now lets (Restrains or hold back) will let, until he be taken out of the way and then shall that "Wicked One" be revealed, whom the Lord shall consume with the spirit of his mouth, and shall destroy with the brightness of his coming: Even him, whose coming is after the working of Satan with all power and signs and lying wonders and with all deceivableness of unrighteousness in them that perish; because they received not the love of the truth, that they might be saved and for this cause God shall send them a strong delusion, that they should believe a lie: that they all might be damned who believed not the truth, but had pleasure in unrighteousness."

Author's Note: God's wrath is to be poured out upon those who serve the "Beast Within", taking pleasure in unrighteousness, not those that love and serve the Lord. God will even send them a strong delusion to be sure they will not repent.

One More Thought…" For the mystery of iniquity does already work: only he who now lets will let, until he be taken out of the way." II Thessalonians 2:7… He that lets (or restrains) is the Holy Spirit of God.

Until he is taken out of the way, he will continue to restrain the full expression of evil in human flesh. Because Jesus said he would never leave us comfortless but would be with us even to the end of the age, it only makes sense that when he, the Holy Spirit, is taken, we will be taken with him. (Full Text-John 14:18-28)

To leave us behind and take the Holy Spirit away would be abandonment and contrary to what Jesus said. So, we will go with the Spirit when he goes and that will be before the Antichrist is revealed. This qualifies us to receive a Pre-Tribulation Exit. The wrath of God falls only after the "Man of Sin" is revealed.

So, Who Will Be Left Behind?

If you are not," Born Again" you will be left behind when the Holy Spirit is taken. You will have to face the anger of the "Antichrist" as he takes over the world and dominates the human race. It will be a full manifestation of evil that the world has never seen. You will be left to go through the 7-year tribulation and be forced to receive the mark of the beast or die. You will be among those that God's wrath will be poured out upon.

However, you still have free will choices to accept Jesus now before it is too late. Once it is too late, you will be under the judgment of God because you rejected the truth all your life.

Those that rejected God to follow false gods, and those that would not submit to the will of God but follows after wickedness…the scripture says God will send them a strong delusion so that they might be damned.

The prevailing notion is that all believers will make it to heaven. But is this theory really grounded in Scripture? I'm convinced that not all believers will be in the rapture. Here's why:

The word, "believe" is defined as: Relying Upon, Adhering To and Trusting In. You can say that you believe but if you are not relying on, adhering to and trusting in, you are not believing. You're just saying you are and fooling yourself.

Examples:

1. I can believe that a chair can support my weight but until I sit down in it, I haven't really believed at all. I had the head knowledge but not the practical relationship. So it is with many Christians. They have head knowledge but no relationship. They do not really believe at all.
2. Many Christians are Christians because they belong to a church

and are relying on their church membership to save them. They do not really know Jesus.

3. Yet other Christians do not follow the doctrine of "Salvation By Grace". They believe in salvation as a result of being good and doing the right things in life. They are never sure of their salvation because it is based upon works, not grace, which is not Biblical. (See Ephesians 2:8-10)

4. Some Christians have fallen for false doctrines that come from Satan that denies Jesus as the Son of God and say that the cross has no bearing on salvation. In effect, they say there are many paths to heaven and eternal life.

5. Other folks start churches based upon false doctrine and capture the souls of those that refuse to follow sound Biblical teaching. Among these churches are The Universal Church, Mormonism, Jehovah's Witness, The Church of Satan, The Gay & Lesbian Church and many others.

I am sure you will come across more than what I have listed. The point is…not all who call themselves Christian will be taken in the rapture of the church. That experience is reserved for true believers that are, "Born Again' and are walking with the Lord. I believe that these true Christians are found in every walk of life and in most every church.

CHAPTER EIGHT:
THE GOD-MAN AND THE DAY OF JUDGMENT

Most of us believe in a, "Judgment Day," a day sometime in the future when God will judge humanity, one by one, for its deeds done in the flesh.

However, more and more, folks are setting aside the notion of divine judgment and the concept of God with it. It's easier to believe in evolution or a pantheistic view of God than to become subject to divine judgment.

If there is a god that is everything and everything is God, there is no need for judgment. If evolution is really true, we are our own gods, ever evolving towards perfection.

On the other hand, if there is only one true and living God, that created us and everything else, we are obligated to find out who God is and what he is like so we don't make him angry.

The Bible tells us that there is only one God and that he did in fact create us along with all of creation. It also says that we are responsible to him and are held accountable.

Humanity is God's greatest work of creation. It is his prize possession. We are the apple of his eye. Genesis tells us that he created us in his own image and his own likeness. We were fashioned in innocence and were being groomed for eternal perfection as a morally righteous being fashioned in the image of God.

"But God commanded his love toward us, in that, while we were yet sinners, Christ died for us" Romans 5:8

So here we sit today waiting to exhale and meet our maker face to face on "Judgment Day." Our merging with God can be a joyful thing but not merging can be a time of terror. The deciding factor is what we did with the plan of Salvation that God gave us.

"For God so loved the world, that he gave his only begotten Son, that whosoever believeth in him should not perish, but have everlasting life." John 3:16

Let's look at some of the divine judgments recorded in the Bible and see if we can learn from them.

OUR ATTITUDE REFLECTS OUR POSTURE

I want to be clear about judgments so before I begin with the judgments of God, I want to discuss judgment in general so we do not get man's judgments confused with those that come from God.

We all know that when we get mad at the government or another individual, we usually formulate a pattern of judgmental speech that delivers condemnation. Our attitude reflects our judgmental posture and we can see that in ourselves and in others. Sometimes we fluff it off as being from God so as to justify our actions.

This was the case with the white supremacy folks in the south during the race riots. They used the Bible, twisting its meanings to validate their actions. We also saw this in WWII with the Nazis'. They declared God dead and used the absence of God to condemn 29 million people to death including 6-million Jews.

Our desires to kill, condemn, criticize, and gossip are not and can never be divine. All these things are sin and should be put out of our minds as quickly as they enter.

Hear the Word of the Lord:

1. "Dearly beloved, avenge not yourselves, but *rather* give place unto wrath: for it is written, Vengeance *is* mine; I will repay, saith the Lord." Romans 12:19

2. "For we know him that hath said, Vengeance *belongs* unto me, I will recompense, saith the Lord. And again, The Lord shall judge his people." Hebrews 10:30

3. "'Vengeance is Mine, and retribution, in due time their foot will slip; For the day of their calamity is near and the impending things are hastening upon them." Deuteronomy 32:35

4. "Do not say, "Thus I shall do to him as he has done to me; I will render to the man according to" his work." Proverbs 24:29

5. "May the LORD judge between you and me, and may the LORD avenge me on you; but my hand shall not be against you." I Samuel 24:12

NATURAL DISASTERS

I know what you're thinking…what about so called "Acts of God?" Things like Earthquakes, Floods, Tornadoes and other events that are beyond our control?

An "Act of God" is an insurance term. It is an event that is caused solely by the effect of nature or natural causes and without any interference by humans whatsoever.

Why do we automatically assume that a hurricane or flood is a direct act of God? The Bible says, "For we know that the whole creation groans and travails in pain together until now." Romans 8:22

The whole creation is in a state of turmoil. No wonder there are violent acts of nature occurring around the world. That is not to say that they are a direct and vicious attack by God.

We have already seen the nature of God through his attributes and how he is compassionate, merciful, loving…all of which are good. The so-called "Acts of God" would be out of character. They do not line up with who God is and his care for mankind.

So, what do we do when bad things happen to us? Here are a few thoughts.

1. Seek the Lord, applying Proverbs 3:5-6… ("Trust in the LORD with all thine heart; and lean not unto thine own understanding. In all thy ways acknowledge him, and he shall direct thy paths.") No matter what has happened, God will direct your paths if you trust in him. He will lead you out of the sorrow, stress and heartaches.
2. Let the Lord comfort you. ("Blessed be God, even the Father of our Lord Jesus Christ, the Father of mercies, and the God of all comfort") II Corinthians 1:3
3. Know that Jesus is always with you. ("lo, I am with you always, even unto the end of the world. Amen." Matthew 28:20b
4. Realize that God will work everything together for good. ("And we know that all things work together for good to them that love God, to them who are the called according to his purpose.") Romans 8:28
5. Refocus your eyes upon those things that you cannot see for they are eternal. "While we look not at the things which are seen, but at the things which are not seen: for the things which are seen *are* temporal; but the things which are not seen *are* eternal." II Corinthians 4:18
6. Rest in the Lord, knowing that He will deliver you. ("The angel of the LORD encamps round about them that fear him, and deliverers them.") Psalm 34:7

Natural disasters are just that…a natural result of a creation that is in turmoil. They are not planned by God as an act of vengeance. I am referring to God's Children when I say all that I said above.

NATURAL DISASTERS AND THE CHILDREN OF DARKNESS

It's a different story if you are a child of the devil. God will and has used natural and even supernatural weather events to carry out his vengeance against the children of darkness.

When God uses the elements of nature in judgment, he does it with such a splendor that everyone knows it was him. There is no doubt or question.

All I have to do is mention the great Deluge or Flood or the two cities of Sodom and Gomorrah where they were destroyed when God rained down fire and brimstone from heaven. It's important to note that God's judgments always fall on the wicked. He never pours out his wrath on his children.

He will however, allow the overthrow of his people by wicked kings because his children have turned away to follow false gods. The Old Testament is full of situations where the people of God began to worship idols. As a result, they lost their land, homes, wealth, and social status and were even led into captivity by their enemies.

WEATHER, AS GOD'S JUDGMENT MOST RELEVANT VERSES

Joshua 10:11 …As they fled from before Israel, while they were at the descent of Beth-horon, the LORD threw large stones from heaven on them as far as Azekah, and they died; there were more who died from the hailstones than those whom the sons of Israel killed with the sword.

Isaiah 30:30…And the LORD will cause his voice of authority to be heard, And the descending of his arm to be seen in fierce anger, And in the flame of a consuming fire in cloudburst, downpour and hailstones.

Ezekiel 38:22 …"With pestilence and with blood I will enter into judgment with him; and I will rain on him and on his troops, and on the many peoples who are with him, a torrential rain, with hailstones, fire and brimstone.

1 Kings 17:1 ...Now Elijah the Tishbite, who was of the settlers of Gilead, said to Ahab, "As the LORD, the God of Israel lives, before whom I stand, surely there shall be neither dew nor rain these years, except by my word."

Haggai 1:10-11 ..."Therefore, because of you the sky has withheld its dew and the earth has withheld its produce. "I called for a drought on the land, on the mountains, on the grain, on the new wine, on the oil, on what the ground produces, on men, on cattle and on all the labor of your hands."

Genesis 7:11-12 ...In the six hundredth year of Noah's life, in the second month, on the seventeenth day of the month, on the same day all the fountains of the great deep burst open, and the floodgates of the sky were opened. The rain fell upon the earth for forty days and forty nights.

Exodus 9:22-26 ...Now the LORD said to Moses, "Stretch out your hand toward the sky, that hail may fall on all the land of Egypt, on man and on beast and on every plant of the field, throughout the land of Egypt." Moses stretched out his staff toward the sky, and the LORD sent thunder and hail, and fire ran down to the earth. And the LORD rained hail on the land of Egypt. So, there was hail, and fire flashing continually in the midst of the hail, very severe, such as had not been in all the land of Egypt since it became a nation.

Leviticus 26:18-19 ...'If also after these things you do not obey me, then I will punish you seven times more for your sins. 'I will also break down your pride of power; I will also make your sky like iron and your earth like bronze.

Deuteronomy 11:17 ..."Or the anger of the LORD will be kindled against you, and he will shut up the heavens so that there will be no rain and the ground will not yield its fruit; and you will perish quickly from the good land which the LORD is giving you.

Deuteronomy 28:22-24 ..."The LORD will smite you with consumption and with fever and with inflammation and with fiery heat and with the sword and with blight and with mildew, and they will pursue you until you perish. "The heaven which is over your head shall be bronze, and the earth which is under you, iron. "The LORD will make the rain of your land powder and dust; from heaven it shall come down on you until you are destroyed.

Jeremiah 3:3 ..."Therefore the showers have been withheld and there has been no spring rain Yet you had a harlot's forehead; You refused to be ashamed.

Jeremiah 14:1-6 ...That which came as the word of the LORD to Jeremiah in regard to the drought: "Judah mourns and her gates languish; They sit on the ground in mourning, And the cry of Jerusalem has ascended. "Their nobles have sent their servants for water; They have come to the cisterns and found no water They have returned with their vessels empty; They have been put to shame and humiliated and they cover their heads.

Amos 4:7 ..."Furthermore, I withheld the rain from you while there were still three months until harvest. Then I would send rain on one city and on another city, I would not send rain; One part would be rained on, while the part not rained on would dry up.

Zechariah 14:17-19 ...And it will be that whichever of the families of the earth does not go up to Jerusalem to worship the King, the LORD of hosts, there will be no rain on them. If the family of Egypt does not go up or enter, then no rain will fall on them; it will be the plague with which the LORD smites the nations who do not go up to celebrate the Feast of Booths. This will be the punishment of Egypt, and the punishment of all the nations who do not go up to celebrate the Feast of Booths.

Job 30:15 ..."Terrors are turned against me; They pursue my honor as the wind, and my prosperity has passed away like a cloud.

Jeremiah 23:19 ..."Behold, the storm of the LORD has gone forth in wrath, even a whirling tempest; It will swirl down on the head of the wicked.

Isaiah 55:10-11…"For as the rain and the snow come down from heaven and do not return there without watering the earth and making it bear and sprout and furnishing seed to the sower and bread to the eater; So will my word be which goes forth from my mouth; It will not return to me empty, without accomplishing what I desire and without succeeding in the matter for which I sent it.

Let's look at some of the Judgments of God. I see them in 10 categories:

1. Judgments against nations.
2. Judgments against cities.
3. Judgments against individuals.
4. Judgments against angels.
5. Judgments against demons.
6. Judgments against the redeemed.
7. Judgments against the lost or un-saved.
8. Judgments against sin.
9. The Great White Throne Judgment.
10. The judgment of the damned

WHAT GOD DOES TO SINFUL NATIONS

The Bible and history show that God will destroy the sinful nations that forget him. *Psalm 9:17* says, "The wicked shall be turned into hell, and all the nations that forget God." Every nation will be judged in its proper time. Since God has promised to warn the sinful nation before it happens. There is a time for everything and the time to repent is now before it is too late.

The Bible has many examples of people trying to repent after judgment began but God did not accept them because they did not repent when God called them to repentance. By not repenting at the proper time, you run the risk of not being accepted by God.

Here are a few nations that were destroyed by God's Wrath because of their evil and wickedness: Persia, Philistines, Ephraim, Amalekites, Hittites, Jebusites, Moabites, Israel, Canaanites, Assyria, Rome and all the nations at the time of the flood. You will discover more as you read more on the subject.

Jeremiah 11:11,14 says:

- Therefore, thus saith the LORD, Behold, I will bring evil upon them, which they shall not be able to escape; and though they shall cry unto me, I will not hearken unto them.
- Therefore pray not thou for this people, neither lift up a cry or prayer for them: for I will not hear them in the time that they cry unto me for their trouble.
- *Jeremiah 8:5,7* **says:**
- They refuse to return (repent).... no man repented him of his wickedness, saying, what have I done? Every one turned to his course, as the horse rushes into the battle.
- Yea, the stork in the heaven knows her appointed times; and the turtle and the crane and the swallow observe the time of their coming; but my people know not the judgment of the LORD.

God says the animals know when to do certain things but the people don't know when it's time to repent.

WHAT ABOUT AMERICA?

Psalm 9:17 says "The wicked shall be turned into hell, and all the nations that forget God." This is a promise from God, given thousands of years ago through a prophetic word. It still applies today as it was then.

The Sins of America... Here is a partial list of the sins of America that provokes God to bring judgment: ***"Woe To Them That Call Evil Good And Good Evil"***

Abortion... Our Nation is stained with the innocent blood of abortion and because no one will acknowledge it as sin and repent, it cannot be cleansed. Simple Mathematics Shows How Much Innocent Blood America Will Have to Answer For...Just like the prophet Nahum said of ancient Nineveh, people in America are continually stumbling upon murder victims. These victims are the unborn that are killed every day, now totaling *over 60 million.*

The primary guilt is not with politicians or judges or abortion providers, but with the mothers who allow themselves to be deceived and believe the lies of the abortion providers whose goal is to make a profit.

They are the ones that know better but still engage the services of someone, "the Government Funded clinic" to murder their unborn children. Also everyone who agrees with, consents to, or otherwise does not oppose abortion bears part of the guilt. You must stand against and speak against abortion or you will bear part of the guilt. If you say it should be left to the mother to decide, then you favor abortion.

Fornication and Adultery-This nation has gone crazy over sex. Even Christian ministries give an inordinate amount of attention to sex and marriage. In Old Testament times adultery got the death penalty, thus showing how God considers this a grievous sin. There are countless scriptures that condemn all kinds of sexual impurity.

Homosexuality... It is still a sin according to the Bible. Some people think this sin has evolved into "not sin." Stealing, lying, murder, adultery, robbery are still sins. They have not evolved into "not sin." The Bible teaches against all forms of sexual impurity.

Covetousness-This is when you never have enough money. Covetous people sit around and talk about what they "need." They make lists of things they want to buy. They imagine themselves winning the lottery. They always want the next gadget that comes along. When people have an income and still never have enough money, the root cause of their problem most often is covetousness. Covetous or greedy people are always in a financial bind. In Romans 1:29 the apostle Paul makes a list of sins and covetousness is right in among fornication and murder.

1. **Romans 1:29…** "Being filled with all unrighteousness, fornication, wickedness, covetousness, maliciousness; full of envy murder, debate deceit, malignity; whisperers,"

2. **1Timothy 6:9-10…** "But they that will be rich fall into temptation and a snare, and into many foolish and hurtful lusts, which drown men in destruction and perdition: For the love of money is the root of all-evil: which while some coveted after, they have erred from the faith, and pierced themselves through with many sorrows."

3. **Jeremiah 6:13…** "For from the least of them even unto the greatest of them every one is given to covetousness; and from the prophet even unto the priest every one deals falsely."

4. **Jeremiah 22:15-17….** "Shalt thou reign, because thou closest thyself in cedar? did not thy father eat and drink, and do judgment and justice, and then it was well with him? He judged the cause of the poor and needy; then it was well with him: was not this to know me? saith the LORD. But thine eyes and thine heart are not but for thy covetousness, and for to shed innocent blood, and for oppression, and for violence, to do it."

Do you see in verse 17 above how covetousness is mixed up with shedding innocent blood, oppression, and violence? It is not a light thing to be covetous. The Bible says we should hate covetousness. (Exodus 18:21)

The above references fit America perfectly. The warnings from God have been sent from heaven and are still being sent. If we do not repent, our nation will be dragged into hell as the scripture says in Psalm 9:17. God help us to repent before it's too late.

CITY STATES THAT FELL

UNDER GOD'S WRATH

Here's a partial list of cities that God dealt with because of sin and wickedness; Sodom & Gomorrah, Babylon, Canaan, Petra, Edom, Jericho, Moab, Philistia, Dumah, Tyre and Damascus and let's not forget Jerusalem.

You probably have never heard of many of these cities. That is because they were dragged into hell and no trace was left of them save a dim historical mention.

You can study every nation, every kingdom and every society in the cities of God's Wrath and you will see the common denominators that all of them had…Immorality, Idolatry, and Sexual Perversion. *These are the embers that flame the fires of God's Wrath.*

THE DEAD WILL FACE THE JUDGMENT OF ALL-MIGHTY GOD

"And I saw a great white throne, and him that sat on it, from whose face the earth and the heaven fled away; and there was found no place for them: and I saw the dead, small and great, stand before God; and the books were opened: and another book was opened, which is the book of life: and the dead were judged out of those things which were written in the books, according to their works: and the sea gave up the dead, which were in it; and death and hell delivered up the dead, which were in them: and they were judged every man according to their works: and death and hell were cast into the lake of fire.

This is the second death: and whosoever was not found written in the book of life was cast into the lake of fire."

Revelation 20:11-15 …We have a date with God in eternity to discuss our future. And as it is appointed unto men once to die, but after this the judgment: Hebrews 9:27 "For God hath not appointed us to wrath, but to obtain salvation by our Lord Jesus Christ" I Thessalonians 5:9

The judge that you appear before, out there in eternity, will be one of mercy or of wrath. We pick the Judge on this side of life. After death, we will meet God face to face. There are two thrones where judgment takes place, The *Great White Throne judgment* and the **"*Bema Seat.*"** All of humanity will meet with Jesus at one of these thrones. No one is exempt.

Peter told the early church that they, because they were followers of Christ, would not be invited to the Throne of his wrath. John, who wrote the book of Revelation, tells us that the dead, small and great…everyone would have to stand before God at the Great White Throne Judgment.

The reason followers of Christ will not be there is because it is for the dead and Christians have been "Born Again" and are alive forever more.

Life is to be in relationship with Jesus.

THE DIFFERENCE BETWEEN THE GREAT WHITE THRONE AND THE BEMA OR JUDGMENT SEAT

The Great White Throne Judgment is where all the dead are summoned to be judged. All are judged by what was written in the books that were opened. Their deeds are on trial.

Another book was also opened, the book of Life. Those whose name was not found written in the "Book of Life" were cast into the lake of fire. Thus occurs the second death. The 1st death being physical and the 2nd death spiritual which lasts forever.

The Judgment Seat of Christ, or "**Bema Seat**" is where followers of Christ are rewarded for their loyalty to him while in the flesh. "For we must all appear before the judgment seat of Christ; that every one may receive the things *done* in *his* body, according to that he hath done, whether *it be* good or bad." II Corinthian 5:10

The difference in the two judgments is, one is a true judgment that administers punishment for things done in the flesh. The other is where followers receive awards and honor for their faith and commitment to Christ.

THE MEANING OF THE JUDGMENT (BEMA) SEAT

Both Romans 14:10 and 2 Corinthians 5:9 speak of the "judgment seat." This is a translation of one Greek word, the word *bema*. While *bema* is used in the gospels and Acts of the raised platform where a Roman magistrate or ruler sat to make decisions and pass sentence (Matt. 27:19; John 19:13), its use in the epistles by Paul, because of his many allusions to the Greek athletic contests, is more in keeping with its original use among the Greeks.

This word was taken from Isthmian games where the contestants would compete for the prize under the careful scrutiny of judges who would make sure that every rule of the contest was obeyed (2 Tim. 2:5). The victor of a given event who participated according to the rules was led by the judge to the platform called the *Bema*. There the laurel wreath was placed on his head as a symbol of victory (1 Cor. 9:24-25).

In all of these passages, "Paul was picturing the believer as a competitor in a spiritual contest.

As the victorious Grecian athlete appeared before the *Bema* to receive his perishable award, so the Christian will appear before Christ's *Bema* to receive his imperishable award. The judge at the *Bema* bestowed rewards to the victors. He did not whip the losers." We might add, neither did he sentence them to hard labor.

In other words, it is a reward seat and portrays a receiving of rewards or a loss of rewards following examination, but it is not a time of punishment where believers are judged for their sins. Such would be inconsistent with the finished work of Christ on the Cross-because he totally paid the penalty for our sins.

With reference to sin, Scripture teaches that the child of God under grace shall not come into judgment (John 3:18; 5:24; 6:37; Rom. 5:1; 8:1; 1 Cor. 11:32); in his standing before God, and on the ground that the penalty for all sin—past, present, and future (Col. 2:13)—has been borne by Christ as the perfect Substitute, the believer is not only placed beyond condemnation, but being in Christ is accepted in the perfection of Christ (1Cor. 1:30; Eph. 1:6; Col. 2:10; Heb. 10:14) and loved of God as Christ is loved (John 17:23).

THE POSITIVE ASPECTS OF THE BEMA

(1) To evaluate the quality of every believer's work whether it is good or bad, i.e., acceptable and thus worthy of rewards, or unacceptable, to be rejected and unworthy of rewards. Actually, an evaluation is going on every day by the Lord (Rev. 2-3).

(2) To destroy and remove unacceptable production portrayed in the symbols of wood, hay, and stubble. All sinful deeds, thoughts, and motives, as well as all good deeds done in the energy of the flesh will be consumed like wood, hay, and stubble before a fire because they are unworthy of reward.

(3) To reward the believer for all the good he or she has done as portrayed by the symbols of gold, silver, and precious stones, that which is valuable and can stand the test of fire without being consumed. 1 Cor. 3:13-15 says each man's work will become evident; for the day will show it, because it is *to be* revealed with fire; and the fire itself will test the quality of each man's work.

If any man's work which he has built upon it remains, he shall receive a reward. If any man's work is burned up, he shall suffer loss; but he himself shall be saved, yet so as through fire.

Therefore, do not go on passing judgment before the time, *but wait* until the Lord comes who will both bring to light the things hidden in the darkness and disclose the motives of *men's* hearts; and then each man's praise will come to him from God.

The Lord will evaluate the quality and nature of every person's work. Compare also:

2 Corinthians 5:10…"For we must all appear before the judgment seat of Christ, that each one may be recompensed for his deeds in the body, according to what he has done, whether good or bad."

Revelation 22:12 … "Behold, I am coming quickly, and my reward *is* with me, to render to every man according to what he has done."

THE NEGATIVE ASPECTS OF THE BEMA

There are a number of passages that refer to the negative aspects of the *Bema* which need to be mentioned and explained. In these passages we read such things as "give account of himself," "suffer loss," "shrink away from him in shame," and "recompense for his deeds … whether good or bad."

Will believers experience shame, grief, and remorse at the *Bema*? If so, how do we reconcile this with passages like Revelation 7:17, "God shall wipe away every tear from their eye," and Revelation 21:4, "and he shall wipe away every tear from their eyes; and there shall no longer be any death; there shall no longer be any mourning, or crying, or pain; the first things have passed away," or with Isaiah 65:17, "For behold, I create new heavens and a new earth; And the former things shall not be remembered or come to mind"?

THE NEGATIVE EFFECTS INVOLVE THE FOLLOWING:

(1) The loss suffered in 1 Corinthians 3:15 refers to the loss of rewards, not salvation as the verse goes on to make clear. Please note that the clause "he shall suffer loss" would be better rendered "it (the reward) shall be forfeited."

(2) The disqualification mentioned in 1 Corinthians 9:27 means disqualified from rewards, not loss of salvation. This is clear from the context and the analogy to the Greek athletic games.

(3) The "recompense" (NASB) or the "receive back" (KJV) of 2 Corinthians 5:10 refers to the dispensing of rewards or their loss. The verb used is *komizo* and means "to carry off safe," "to carry off as booty." In the middle voice as here, it meant "to bear for oneself," or "to receive back what is one's own." Compare Matthew 25:27 and Ephesians 6:8.

(4) That dispensing of rewards is in view is also evident from the Greek words in 2 Corinthians 5:10 translated "good" (*agathos*—valuable like good fruit) and "bad" (*phaulos*—unacceptable like rotten or spoiled fruit).

This is no more a punishment than when a student turns in a worthless assignment and receives an F or a D. His poor work results in a just grade or recompense. This is what his work deserves. There used to be a sign in the registrar's office at Dallas Seminary, which read, "Salvation is by grace … Graduation is by works."

(5) *1 John 2:28*. This verse undoubtedly refers to the *Bema* and shows there will be both boldness as a result of abiding, and shame before the Lord as a result of failing to abide. "And now little children." John is writing to believers. This is his term of endearment for his readers as born-again people.

"Abide in Him." "Abide" is a synonym for fellowship which is the subject of the book (1:3-7). It means to remain in him from the standpoint of drawing on his life as the source of ours and then to obey him out of that relationship of dependence.

This is the basis of rewards or the cause of their loss, the abiding, Christ-dependent life. "So that" points us to the purpose, the return of the Savior and what it will mean.

"When he appears."

The "when" points to the imminency of the return of the Lord. It is literally "if he appears." The conditional clause does not question the reality of Christ's coming, only the time of it and thereby points to its imminency. "Appears" refers to the rapture, which leads quickly into the *Bema*. (Taken from Bible.org Article)

So, here's what we know from our study so far:

1. Believers are rewarded for their faith and dedication at the Judgment Seat of Christ.
2. Non-believers are judged in accordance to their works. However, all that are not found in the Lamb's Book of Life are cast into the Lake of Fire.
3. No non-believer escapes Judgment Day. Judgment is an appointment after we die.
4. Christians are not included with the lost on the day of Judgment. They escape the wrath of God because Jesus bore it in his body for them and they accepted his finished work of Grace.

THE JUDGMENT AGAINST ANGELS & DEMONS

Fallen angels are those that rebelled against God to follow Lucifer, which we also know as Satan and the devil or evil one. They were thrown out of heaven. The angels became demons and now dwell in a disembodied state as an evil spirit under an eternal chain of darkness.

"And the angels which kept not their first estate, but left their own habitation, he hath reserved in everlasting chains under darkness unto the judgment of the great day." Jude 1:6

He hath reserved in everlasting chains - 2 Peter 2:4. Peter says, "chains of darkness;" that is, the darkness encompasses them "as" chains. Jude says that those chains are "everlasting."

The sense is, that that deep darkness always endures; there is no intermission; no light; it will exist forever. This passage in itself does not prove that the punishment of the rebel angels will be eternal, but merely that they are kept in a dark prison in which there is no light, and which is to exist for ever, with reference to the final trial.

The punishment of the rebel angels after the judgment is represented as an everlasting fire, which has been prepared for them and their followers, Matthew 25:41. (Excerpts from Barns Commentary Notes)

The only way to see the light of day is through your eyes. If that evil spirit can influence you and attach itself to you, it can see and with that sight, live again to bring torment to your soul and death to your dreams and hopes for the future. That's why Jesus defeated all of them on the cross and has given us the spiritual weapons to protect ourselves from demonic attacks.

The Serpent Bites The Dust... Genesis... 3:14-15 tells us about the judgment of the Serpent that was used by Satan to bring down Adam & Eve. The LORD God said to the serpent, "Because you have done this, cursed are you more than all cattle and more than every beast of the field; On your belly you will go and dust you will eat all the days of your life; and I will put enmity between you and the woman and between your seed and her seed; He shall bruise you on the head and you shall bruise him on the heel."

This is the 1st prophecy of the Messiah and God himself uttered it. He said that the serpent, now being referred to as Satan, would bruise his, Jesus' heel but Jesus would crush his, the serpent (devil's) head. This happened by Jesus on the cross and was recorded for our edification.

Author's Note: "Messiah" is an Old Testament Hebrew word for Anointed. The word Christ is a New Testament Greek word for Anointed.)

"And having spoiled principalities and powers, he made a shew of them openly, triumphing over them in it. Colossians 2:15

Judgment of This World... 2 Peter 3:7 "But by his word the present heavens and earth are being reserved for fire, kept for the day of judgment and destruction of ungodly men. "

HERE ARE SOME MORE REFERENCES TO THE DESTRUCTION OF OUR EARTH

Genesis 6:13 ...Then God said to Noah, "The end of all flesh has come before me; for the earth is filled with violence because of them; and behold, I am about to destroy them with the earth.

Mark 13:31 ..."Heaven and earth will pass away, but my words will not pass away.

Revelation 21:1... Then I saw a new heaven and a new earth; for the first heaven and the first earth passed away, and there is no longer any sea. Isaiah 51:6 ..."Lift up your eyes to the sky, then look to the earth beneath; For the sky will vanish like smoke, and the earth will wear out like a garment and its inhabitants will die in like manner; But my salvation will be forever and my righteousness will not wane.

Zephaniah 1:18...Neither their silver nor their gold will be able to deliver them on the day of the LORD'S wrath; And all the earth will be devoured In the fire of his jealousy, For he will make a complete end, indeed a terrifying one, of all the inhabitants of the earth.

Isaiah 34:4 ...And all the host of heaven will wear away and the sky will be rolled up like a scroll; All their hosts will also wither away as a leaf withers from the vine, as one withers from the fig tree.

Matthew 5:18…"For truly I say to you, until heaven and earth pass away, not the smallest letter or stroke shall pass from the Law until all is accomplished.

Matthew 24:29…"But immediately after the tribulation of those days THE SUN WILL BE DARKENED, AND THE MOON WILL NOT GIVE ITS LIGHT, AND THE STARS WILL FALL from the sky, and the powers of the heavens will be shaken.

2 Peter 3:10…But the day of the Lord will come like a thief, in which the heavens will pass away with a roar and the elements will be destroyed with intense heat, and the earth and its works will be burned up.

2 Peter 3:12 …looking for and hastening the coming of the day of God, because of which the heavens will be destroyed by burning, and the elements will melt with intense heat!

Revelation 6:14…The sky was split apart like a scroll when it is rolled up and every mountain and island were moved out of their places.

Revelation 20:11… Then I saw a great white throne and him who sat upon it, from whose presence earth and heaven fled away and no place was found for them.

Revelation 8:7…The first sounded, and there came hail and fire, mixed with blood and they were thrown to the earth; and a third of the earth was burned up and a third of the trees were burned up and all the green grass was burned up.

GOD'S JUDGMENT AGAINST SIN

Romans 5:12-17 tells us, "Wherefore, as by one man sin entered into the world, and *death by sin;* and so death passed upon all men, for that all have sinned: (For until the law sin was in the world: but sin is not imputed when there is no law. Nevertheless, death reigned from Adam to Moses, even over them that had not sinned after the similitude of Adam's transgression, who is the figure of him that was to come.

But not as the offence, so also is the free gift. For if through the offence of one many be dead, much more the grace of God, and the gift by grace, which is by one man, Jesus Christ, hath abounded unto many. And not as it was by one that sinned, so is the gift: for the judgment was by one to condemnation, but the free gift is of many offences unto justification; For if by one man's offence death reigned by one; much more they which receive abundance of grace and of the gift of righteousness shall reign in life by one, Jesus Christ.)

Romans 8:3... give us a clearer picture of God's Judgment of sin. "For what the law could not do, in that it was weak through the flesh, God sending his own Son in the likeness of sinful flesh, and for sin, condemned sin in the flesh:"

Jesus paid the penalty for our sin. All the sins of the entire world were laid upon him. God judged Sin in the flesh but not any flesh. The only flesh that could be judged is the flesh of Jesus because his flesh was holy, righteous and pure. There was no sin in him. That's why we call him the slain Lamb of God. He was foreshadowed in the sacrificial system of Israel where the pure Lamb was slain for the sins of the people. Year after year this happened until Jesus came. He was the purest of them all and it took just one to die for sin.

Romans 5;10 further clarifies this, "For if, when we were enemies, we were reconciled to God by the death of his Son, much more, being reconciled, we shall be saved by his life."

His death paid the penalty but his life, because it was and is holy and righteous, saves us. That means when I feel bad about myself or unworthy in any way, I can look to Jesus by faith and declare that his righteousness is now mine and I can finally have a life above criticism, hostility and hatred…so says the apostle Paul to the Galatians 2:20

"I am crucified with Christ: nevertheless, I live; yet not I, but Christ lives in me: and the life which I now live in the flesh I live by the faith of the Son of God, who loved me, and gave himself for me."

We have looked at a lot of divine Judgments, those against Nations,

Cities, People, Angels and Demons, Satan and others. We looked at "The Day of Judgment" and if and when God's children are judged by God. We looked at the "Judgment Seat of Christ" and what is and what it is not.

Without exception, the verses reviewed declare that God's wrath will fall on the ungodly, not the righteous. Therefore, to escape the terrible day of vengeance that God will bring upon this world, we need only to repent, believe in Christ as the penalty for sin, and put our faith in his finished work of Grace.

As long as we do not follow the example of the Old Testament Saints that fell into immorality and followed after false gods, we will never experience God's wrath.

We surely do not want to be accounted with the damned. God is able and willing to bring us out of temptation and snares set for us by the devil. He wants us to walk by faith with him.

CONCLUSION

Well, there you have it. The life and destiny of the God-Man is a fantastic true story that spans many generations. It encompasses man's fall from God's favor to being rescued by God, restored and destined for greatness.

The God-Man began with Adam, finished with Christ and now, in these last days, continues with every "Born Again" believer.

The God-Man is simply man, (or Woman) filled with God. This allows God to rule in his children's hearts and bring forth his image and likeness back to the earth once again.

What was lost in Adam was redeemed in Jesus and now lives in us, his followers. We are the beneficiaries of his love and grace.

The God-Man can now approach the very throne of God without being summoned and fellowship with his Heavenly Father. He (She) is a child of God with full family privileges and authority.

Satan broke the link that united God and man through lies and deception but Jesus restored that link, bringing back his image and likeness to mankind. "For the Son of man is come to seek and to save that which was lost." Luke 19:10

The God-Man continues in you, if you are "Born Again." It's time to be the man or woman of God that you were created to be.

> "And the Word is once again made flesh as it dwells in us"

May the Lord bless you and keep you and cause his face to shine upon you and give you peace as you live for him.

ABOUT THE AUTHOR
JOHN MARINELLI

Rev. Marinelli is an ordained minister, He has formed and been pastor of one church in Wisconsin and was the pastor of another in Alabama. He has also been a youth minister and evangelism director over the years.

Rev. Marinelli has authored several other books including: "Original Story Poems", "The Art of Writing Christian Poetry," "Pulpit Poems," "Moonlight & Mistletoe," "The Mysterious Stranger," "With Eagles Wings," "Mysteries & Miracles," "It Came To Pass," Why Do The Righteous Suffer," "Believer's Handbook of battle Strategies." "Hidden In Plain Sight" "The End of The World, From The Beginning, Shadows in the Light of a Pale Moon," "Mister Tugboat" "An Elephant Named Clyde" "Morning Reign" "Times Past But Not Forgotten" "How To Be Happy" and "How To Have A Victorious Christian Life."(www.marinellichristianbooks.com)

John is an accomplished Christian poet. He also dabbles in songwriting, likes to play chess, sings karaoke and goes fishing now and then. He lives in north central Florida where he enjoys a retired lifestyle with his wife and two collies.

GALLERY OF ENCOURAGING CHRISTIAN POEMS

AGREEING WITH GOD

We speak of things that are not,
Believing in them as though they were,
Because our Heavenly Father spoke them first,
Sending them to us in promises that never blur.

We take Him at His Word,
And listen to all He has to say.
We wrap each promise around our souls,
Until what was spoken becomes our day.

We will agree with the Lord,
Trusting that He knows best.
For only His awesome power,
Can provide our souls with rest.

"As it is written, I have made thee a father of many nations, before Him who he believed, even God who quickens the dead and calls those things that be not as though they were" Romans 4:17

Like Abraham, we also have a destiny that God has spoken into our lives. He calls it forth before it exists. Like Abraham, we are to believe, even against hope, that what God said will indeed come to be. (Romans 4:18).

ARM'S LENGTH

I hold the world at arm's length,
That its choices do not interfere.
While it does its own thing,
I watch and wait over here.

My steps must not go that way,
For it's not where I need to be.
The Lord has shown me the path,
That will lead me to my destiny.

The call of the world is strong
And pulls at me now and then.
But I know that way
Is full of sorrow and sin.

I must move on in life
Beyond their beckoning call.
It's the right thing to do,
So I do not stumble or fall.

I will not be swayed or misled
By family, friends or business deal.
Their secret thoughts are not mine,
To consider, to admire or feel.

So I keep the world at "Arm's Length"
As I journey through this life.
My faith in Jesus keeps me strong,
As I walk in His glorious light.

"Love not the world, neither the things that are in the world. If any man loves the world, the love of the Father is not in him. For all that is in the world, the lust of the flesh, the lust of the eyes and the pride of life, is not of the Father, but of the world. And the world passes away and the lust thereof: But he that doeth the will of God abides forever. I John 2:15-17

It is more important to know God and to follow after Him, than to become entangled in life's lustful traps: for if we were to gain the whole world and lose our own soul, how terrible would that be?

DON'T WORRY

Don't worry about tomorrow.
You did that yesterday.
Go on with your life
And remember always to pray.

Ask and it shall be given to you,
But this great truth you already know.
Rejoice and be happy, why? Because…
Your harvest comes from what you sow.

I will say it again and even more,
Until it becomes very very clear.
Tomorrow will take care of itself,
But worry is another word for fear.

Now here's what I want you to do.
Trust in the Lord and be of good cheer.
Drop the worry from your vocabulary
And cast out that demon of fear.

Worry is the flipside of faith. If you are walking in faith, you are free from worry. Why, because faith hopes in God and trusts that he will be there to meet your need.

TWO HOUSES

We built our homes together,
Mine upon a Rock and his in the sand.
He thought his would be all right,
But he was a foolish man.

God's wisdom showed me the way.
And what I needed to do,
But my foolish neighbor,
Never had a clue.

Then the rains came,
And the winds began to blow.
The storms beat upon our homes,
And we had nowhere to go.

We built our homes together,
My neighbor and me.
Mine is still there upon the Rock,
But his ceased to be.

Wise men and fools both suffer,
The storms that befall mankind.
But those who trust in Jesus
Will always stand the test of time.

Foundation is everything. If you build your life on the Word of God, it will last forever. That's why we strive to be obedient to the will of God. We want his destine and his blessings, no matter what the world system thinks or does.

CLUTTER

Clutter keeps the mind confused,
As images dance through the night.
Lost among those unimportant thoughts,
Are the dreams that once shined bright.

An endless parade of fear and doubt,
Crowds the mind to destroy our day.
Ever soaring on the wings of the soul,
Until it has formed an evil array.

But clutter is by one's choice,
Of those who dance to its beat.
Better to face imaginations' due
Than to fall into utter defeat.

Be Quiet!!! Is our spirit's desperate cry,
As we call upon the name of the Lord.
Silence is our heart's desired prayer,
Until our minds are again restored.

"Keep thy heart with all diligence: for out of it are the issues of life" Proverbs 4:23

We make the final choices in life that either lead us astray or closer to the Lord. We chose what enters our hearts and fills our minds. May we always choose the path of righteousness and the way of peace.

THE LORD'S LITTLE TWO BY FOUR

God has a little 2' X 4'
That rest on heaven's windowsill.
He uses it now and then,
When we stray from His will.

Sometimes we need a good "Bap";
With the Lord's little 2' X 4'
To knock out the confusion,
And help us to desire Him more.

The Lord's little 2' X 4'
Is what we sometimes need,
To get our thinking straight,
And keep our focus indeed.

The Lord's little 2' X 4'
Is fashioned from life's every trial,
So we do not stray from His will,
Or fall into an ungodly lifestyle.

"My son, despise not the chastening of the Lord; neither be weary of His correction: for whom the Lord loves, He corrects; even as a father his son, in whom he delights." Proverbs 3:11 & 12

It is a good thing to be corrected by God. We should not fear His rebuke for it is not His wrath, but rather a blessing from His love that keeps us moving on towards maturity.

I FIND MYSELF IN GOD

I find myself in God.
He is my, "Everything"
I know that He is Lord,
My Life, My Hope, My King.

I find myself in God,
Not the ways of Sin.
Nor do I look to others,
To know who I really am.

I find myself in God,
To whom I bow on bended knee.
He alone is my joy and strength
And where I want to be.

"For we are His workmanship, created in Christ Jesus unto good works, which God hath before ordained, that we should walk in them" Ephesians 2:10

Knowing that we are created in Christ Jesus gives us confidence to walk in Christ, as He walked, along a pathway of good works. It is our joy and pleasure to be like Him. In Him we move and live and have our being.

"I AM" THERE

"I AM" There,
At the end of your broken dreams,
Before the sun rises over your day,
Prior to those tear-filled streams.

"I AM" There,
Down that road of despair,
When all appears to be lost,
And no one seems to care.

"I AM" There,
Over all of life's twists and turns,
When tomorrow is all but gone,
And when you are full of concerns.

"I AM" There,
Sayeth the Lord of Host,
To bring you hope and peace,
And the power of My Holy Ghost.

"I AM" There,
To be sure you make it through,
In the midst of every trial,
To bless your life and deliver you.

"I Am" There

"All power is given unto me in heaven and earth. Go ye therefore and teach all nations, baptizing them in the name of the Father, and of the Son, and of the Holy Ghost: Teaching them to observe all things, whatsoever I have commanded you: and lo, I am with you always, even unto the end of the world." Mathew 28:18-20

The Lord is with us always. He never leaves our side, even when we leave His. In every situation, He is there. It's time to count on His presence and trust in His care.

John Marinelli

SO LISTEN UP

I write this verse that all should know.
What I have to say is like a seed, ready to grow.
So listen up to all I have to say.
It could be the very blessing your heart needs today.

God has not given you a spirit of fear.
Instead, He has offered to dry up every tear.
He really loves you, even though you often fail.
His love and mercy follows you,
Enabling you to be the head and not the tail.
So do not worry or even fret.
That's why Jesus paid sin's awful debt.
Now go on in life to discover its victory
Knowing that Jesus has indeed set you free.

"For God hath not given us the spirit of fear: but of Power and of Love and a sound mine" II Timothy 1:7

There is nothing to fear except fear itself and that spirit has been defeated on the cross. We now have the Spirit of power and love and a sound mind. He will never leave us or forsake us. We are truly free.

WINNING THE BATTLE

We must use the Word of God
To calm emotions that fray.
For the enemy never sleeps,
Until he has led us astray.

So when your emotions overflow
With feelings like depression and fear.
Know this! If you dwell in that place,
You invite the enemy to draw near.

When your emotions rage
With fiery darts aglow,
Stand in the power of the Lord,
Against its awful woe.

And if you get confused
And lost in the storm,
Put your thoughts on trial,
Rejecting all but heaven born.

You can win the battle
That rages within your soul.
By casting down imaginations,
And breaking Satan's hold.

Remember to focus on Jesus,
Holding the world at arm's length.
Lift up your head above the trial,
And the Lord will give you strength.

"For the weapons of our warfare are not carnal but mighty, through God, to the pulling down of strongholds: casting down imaginations and every high thing that exalts itself against the knowledge of God, and bringing into captivity every thought to the obedience of Christ." II Corinthians 10:3-5 The battle is in our minds and we win by putting our thoughts on trial and casting out all that oppose the knowledge of God. This is true victory.

THE LIGHTHOUSE

A lighthouse is a blessing,
To the ships that toss in the sea.
For it shows them the way,
Until they can clearly see.

The rage of an angry storm,
Cannot hide its brilliant light.
Nor can its awesome furry,
Rule as an endless night.

Jesus is the lighthouse,
For those who have gone astray.
The light of His love,
Offers a new and living way.
Jesus is the lighthouse,
When fear and sickness rage.
The light of His love,
Gives hope in difficult days.

So trust in the Lord,
And look for His light.
He alone is "The Lighthouse",
That guides you through the night.

"I am the Way, the Truth, and the Life. No man cometh to the Father but by me" John 14:6

Life holds many dark nights that are full of unexpected storms. Only a deep abiding faith in Jesus Christ will get us through. He is the light of the world. His light keeps us from falling into confusion, sorrow, sickness and demonic oppression.

THE WAY MAKER

Only Jesus can make a way,
Through the difficulties of life.
He alone is Lord and King,
Over life's sorrows and strife.

He is the "Way Maker,"
When there is no visible way.
He will make the way known,
As though it were the light of day.

He will make a way,
For those of humble heart.
He will clear away the rubble,
Restoring what Satan broke apart.
Jesus is the "Way Maker,"
A friend to all who are lost.
He has made the way,
Paying sin's incredible cost.

The way to the Maker,
Is through His only Son.
He alone is the "Way Maker,"
Until life's battles are won.

"Let not your heart be troubled. Ye believe in God, believe also in me. In my father's house are many mansions: If it were not so, I would have told you. I go to prepare a place for you. And if I go and prepare a place for you, I will come again, and receive you unto myself, that where I am, there ye may be also." John 14: 1-3

The Lord is prepared for any emergency. He knows the beginning from the end and has gone before us to prepare a way that we can follow until we see Him face to face.

STINKING THINKING

Stinking thinking, they say,
Is bad for your health.
For it frustrates life's goals,
And denies happiness and wealth.

A right perspective is important,
As we think about everything.
It will either bring us down,
Or cause us to shout and sing.

What we think about these days,
Really does affect our life.
It can cause us to overflow with Joy,
Or fall into depression and strife.

So don't let your thinking,
Stink all the way up to heaven.
Stand in faith before God,
And get rid of that negative leaven.

"Then Jesus said unto them, take heed and beware of the leaven of the Pharisees and the Sadducees" Mathew 16:6

Someone once said, "We are what we think" The Bible says, "As a man thinks, so is he" It is important to concentrate our thinking of those things that are of good report, pure, honest and that will keep us clean of heart.

WISE MEN STILL SEEK HIM

Wise men still seek Him
Who appeared so long ago.
They come now by grace
Through faithful hearts aglow.

Wise men still seek Him
For He is their "Bread of Life."
A sustaining inner strength
Through times of sorrow or strife.

Wise men still seek Him
The Christ of Calvary.
God's only begotten Son
Crucified as Sin's penalty.

Wise men still seek Him
Jesus, God in human array.
King of kings & Lord of lords
Born to earth on Christmas Day.

"Now when Jesus was born in Bethlehem of Judea in the days of Herod the king, behold, there came wise men from the east to Jerusalem, saying, where is he that is born king of the Jews? For we have seen his star in the east and are come to worship him" Mathew 2:1-2

Seeking Jesus is the wisest thing any man, woman or child can do and when we find Him, it is our privilege to bow down and worship Him. This is our journey, our destiny and our life while on this earth.

THE ANGELS CRY HOLY

The Angels cry "Holy,"
While sorrow fills the land.
For God's Judgment Day,
Is to come upon every man.

The Angels cry "Holy,"
While mankind goes astray,
Rejecting the love of God,
To follow his own precarious way.

The Angels cry "Holy,"
Knowing the terror of the Lord,
When all who dwell in sin,
Will suddenly be destroyed.

The Angels cry "Holy,"
Waiting for all things new,
Born of the Holy Spirit,
When God's Judgment is through.

The Angels cry "Holy,"
"Holy is the Lamb,"
Waiting for the children of God,
To join "The Great I AM"

"And one cried unto another and said, "Holy, Holy, Holy, is the Lord of host: the whole earth is full of his glory" Isaiah 6:3

We serve a Holy God that deserves our reverence and homage. The angels know this and worship Him, but man, because of sin, has no real concept of his own creator.

John Marinelli

A HIGHWAY CALLED "HOLINESS"

He places my feet on
A highway called "Holiness,"
That led my soul
To the throne of God.

Amidst the cheers of angels,
I walk, wearing His holy gown.
Onward towards heaven's throne,
While evil cast its awful frown.

My eyes were opened
That I might see.
Both the good and the evil,
That sought after me.

I walk the highway-Holiness
That crosses all of time.
Towards the throne of God,
Leaving this world behind.

"And an highway shall be there, and a way, and it shall be called, the way of holiness; the unclean shall not pass over it; but it shall be for those: the wayfaring men, though fools, shall not err therein. No lion shall be there, nor any ravenous beast shall go up thereon, it shall not be found there, but the redeemed shall walk there. And the redeemed of the Lord shall return, and come to Zion with songs and everlasting joy upon their heads: They shall obtain joy and gladness, and sorrow and sighing shall flee away. " Isaiah 35:8-10

What a privilege to walk the highway of Holiness. It is prepared especially for us, the redeemed, and it is protected from the errors of fools and the snarl of beast and especially the roar of the lion.

CALL UPON THE LORD

When your burdens overwhelm you,
Like a mighty raging sea.
Call upon the Lord, Jesus,
And He will set you free

When your heartaches are many,
And life is difficult to understand.
Call upon the Lord, Jesus.
He will come and hold your hand.

When your friends reject you,
Because you follow after Him,
Call upon the Lord, Jesus.
And keep yourself from sin.

When you fall into depression,
As though it were a giant pit.
Call upon the Lord, Jesus,
Who will restore your joyful wit.

When you're saddened by the day
Feeling lost and all alone.
Call upon the Lord, Jesus,
Who will make His way known.

When you are weary and heavy laden,
Tired from life's many tests.
Call upon the Lord, Jesus,
Who is sure to give you rest.

"Hear my cry; oh God, attend unto my prayer. From the end of the earth,

I will cry unto thee, when my heart is overwhelmed: Lead me to the rock that is higher than I." Psalms 61:1-2

Calling upon the Lord in stressful times is o.k. He wants us to cry to Him and then to trust in Him to watch over His Word to perform it on our behalf.

IT CAME TO PASS

Things often come to pass,
But seldom do they ever last.
They come into our busy day,
For awhile, then pass away.

We hear their voices, loud and clear,
As they arrive and while they are here.
They speak both joy and misery,
Some to you and some to me.

We say, "It came to pass,"
Or say, "It happened so fast."
Down life's beaten path,
Comes both love and wrath.

So say goodbye to sad and blue.
To all that is now troubling you.
For things will come, only to pass,
But God's love will always last.

"And it came to pass in those days…" Luke2:1

These are the times of our lives. We live them, some for good and some for not so good. One thing is for sure, that which comes our way, comes only to pass on by. It is not what happens that is so important, but rather what we do with what we are faced with.

Trusting in the Lord and seeking His guidance will always conquer that which comes to pass.

THE WHOSOEVER SCENARIO

> The "Whosoever" is who so ever,
> Not who so won't, can't or will not.
> The story is as clear as a sunny day.
> God offers a new and living way.
>
> But only those who engage "free will"
> To choose life, faith and obedience,
> Will find salvation for their souls,
> And be cleansed and made whole.
>
> We do the choosing: to accept or deny.
> That is how God set it up to be.
> He made the call to life's "Whosoever",
> That they could live abundantly.

"For God so loved the world, that he gave his only begotten son, that whosoever believeth in him, should not perish but have everlasting life." John 3:16

We are the "Whosoever" in John 3:16, that one day put his or her faith in Christ, believed in Him and now rest in the Lord's love and grace. We have the promise of God that He sent His Son so we could believe and have everlasting life. How great is that?

LITTLE PRISONS

Little prisons await the man with a lustful soul.
Bars of selfishness and pride create dungeons of icy cold.

Prisons of shame and jealousy fill the heart with utter despair.
Bars that separate from God and those that really care.

Stand back! While the doors are tightly closed;
Taking away your life, to wither as a dying rose.

Beware of those little prisons that trap the lustful soul.
Keep yourself free from sin through faith in the Christ of old.

Little prisons need not to be your fate.
It is your choice, Spirit or flesh to date.

"O Foolish Galatians, who hath bewitched you, that ye should not obey the truth, before whose eyes Jesus Christ hath been, evidently set forth, crucified among you? Are you so foolish? Having begun in the Spirit, are you now made perfect in the flesh?

We should always seek to dwell in the Spirit, that we would not emulate the deeds of the flesh. When we fall short, we create "little prisons" that keep us in confusion and away from the blessing of God. It's time to walk in the Spirit and break the prisons that so easily beset us.

John Marinelli

REST MY CHILD

Rest my child, says the Lord.
Take thy peace and be restored.
I have provided, thy mouth to feed.
From the beginning, I knew your need.

Do not worry, fret or even fear,
For, my child, I am always near
To bless thy soul with love and grace,
To be with thee, face to face.

Come, my child, near to my throne.
Do not allow your faith to roam.
For those who will not believe
Can never find rest in times of need.

My Word shall see you through.
My grace I freely give to you
That you should rest, thy soul to keep,
Forever delivered from unbelief.

Resting in the Lord is the best way to stay happy. However, it requires faith and trust in God that he will be there for you when you need him. It's kind of neat to relax when fear and anxiety are knocking at your door.

A WHISPER IN THE WIND

There's a whisper in the wind
That lingers both day and night.
A champion of truth and justice,
By the power of His might.

A word in due season
That echoes from deep within.
A voice out of nowhere,
Reproving the world of sin.

Look there, in the street
And here, by the shores of the sea.
There's a whisper hidden in the wind;
A voice from eternity.

There's a calling from God.
His voice is hidden in the wind.
In a whisper, He speaks to our hearts
With the love and counsel of a friend.

Listen for the Whisper,
All who seek to know.
It is God's Holy Spirit
Telling you which way to go.

"And thine ears shall hear a word behind thee saying, This is the way, walk ye in it, when ye turn to the right hand and when ye turn to the left" Isaiah 30:21

The voice of the Lord is often a still small voice, yet always clear and it never brings confusion. His voice is like a whisper in the wind that brings a peaceful breeze to the heart. The joy of hearing His voice is to know His will and our destiny.

FRAGILE FLOWER RED

As a flower in earthen sod,
I bloom for thee, oh God.
To blossom with the turn of spring;
To be to you, a beautiful thing.

I lift my Fragile Flower Red
Upward from my earthen bed;
To draw light from God above,
Strength and peace and joy and love.

As a flower, I bloom for thee
That passersby may stop and see.
Your fragrance and beauty I am,
Flowered in grace as a man.

As a flower in earthen sod,
I bloom for thee, oh God.
Upward, I lift my head,
As a Fragile Flower Red.

"Be not conformed to this world, but be ye transformed, by the renewing of your mind, that ye may prove what is that good and acceptable and perfect will of God."

When we look to God as our source, we blossom, much like a flower that draws light from the sun. When we blossom, like a flower, we display the glory and beauty of our creator to all who care to stop and look. This is our divine destiny.

Other books by John Marinelli can be viewed and purchased at: www.marinellichristianbooks.com

www.ingramcontent.com/pod-product-compliance
Lightning Source LLC
Chambersburg PA
CBHW020427010526
44118CB00010B/459